Little, Brown and Company
Time Warner Book Group
1271 Avenue of the Americas, New York, NY 10020
Visit our Web site at www.twbookmark.com

First Edition: April 2006

Portions of this book previously appeared, in different form,
in *The Atlantic Monthly* and *The New Yorker*. *Goodnight Moon* © 1947
by Harper & Row. Text © renewed 1975 by Roberta Brown Rauch.
Illustrations © renewed by Edith Hurd, Clement Hurd, John Thacher Hurd,
and George Hellyer, as trustees of the Edith & Clement Hurd 1982 Trust.
Reprinted with permission from HarperCollins Publishers.

Library of Congress Cataloging-in-Publication Data
Flanagan, Caitlin.
  To hell with all that : loving and loathing our inner housewife / Caitlin
Flanagan — 1st ed.
      p.   cm.
  ISBN 0-316-73687-2 (hardcover) / ISBN-13: 978-0-316-73687-9
  1. Housewives — United States.   2. Marriage — United States.
3. Motherhood — United States.   4. Housekeeping — United States.
I. Title.

HQ759.F585   2006
305.43'64'0973 — dc22   2005022516

10   9   8   7   6   5   4   3   2   1

Q-FF

Printed in the United States of America

To Hell with
All That

To Hell with All That

{ Loving *and* Loathing
Our Inner Housewife }

Caitlin Flanagan

Little, Brown and Company
NEW YORK   BOSTON

For Rob, as always;

For Patrick and Conor;

And for Ellen

A new feeling of love for my children and the

father of my children laid the foundation of a

new life and a quite different happiness; and that

life and happiness have lasted to the present time.

— LEO TOLSTOY, "Family Happiness"

Contents

Preface

FEW THINGS IN LIFE are as terrible as closing up the house of one's parents after they have died. There is the simultaneous urge to save everything and to jettison it all. Freud famously observed that the mourner is not to be rushed, that she must be allowed to accomplish her work "piecemeal." A mourner may relinquish her emotional attachment to the loved one's favorite chair one day, but to his winter coat not for several months or even years. But when my sister and I let ourselves into our parents' house a year after my mother died — and just three weeks after my father lay down on a guestroom bed and quietly followed suit — we were not in the business of beginning a years-long breakup with our parents' possessions, charged though they were with associations and even signs of recent use (the book facedown on the bedside table, the sheet of paper rolled into the typewriter).

We lived in distant cities; we were wives and householders with children in school and husbands who relied on us. We arrived armed with the totems of coolheaded efficiency: colored stickers (red for the things that would be shipped to her house in Santa Barbara, yellow for mine in Los Angeles, blue for Goodwill), pads of lined paper (for composing our separate lists), and Hefty bags for the trash. We had three days to do the job, a hotel room in town (sleeping in the house seemed unimaginable), and the jittery, false cheer of two people who have come through a long, difficult stretch together — my mother's death had been one kind of horror, my father's another — and who are determined to put a miserable episode behind them with dispatch.

In an hour we were undone by the task. While cleaning out my mother's desk, my sister accidentally threw away my eleventh-grade report card, a mistake that threw us instantly back upon our child selves — me sobbing over a minor disappointment, her calmly solving the problem, emptying Hefty bags of paperwork onto the laundry-room floor and sifting through their contents until she produced, unharmed, the sainted report card. It was only after I had hand-carried the thing home and taken an unsentimental look at it that I realized it was not one for posterity. The "A–" in Honors English might be nice to show my children one day, but there was no way to produce that "A–" without also revealing the "C+" in Biology and the "B–" in French III. The only remarkable thing about the report card, it turned out, was the fact that my mother had saved it. The slip of paper was not a testament of past academic glory, only of a hard new fact: there was no longer anyone in the world who loved me enough to save my report cards and school pictures and Christmas poems. I wasn't anyone's daughter anymore.

In emptying the house of the recently dead, you gird yourself for certain moments of obvious pathos — the pair of gloves still holding the shape of the hands that wore them — but get continually blindsided by the least resonant objects imaginable. The work is hampered by the fact that holding on to a comprehensive and inflexible understanding that the loved one is really and truly kaput is very difficult in the early weeks. Clearly my father didn't need his body anymore (what a fiasco), but I had to stand at his closet for twenty minutes convincing myself that he was also no longer in need of his oxblood loafers, practically new and recently shined. The little yellow teapot was not hard to confront; taking off its lid and finding a twenty-dollar bill tucked inside meant discovering anew that something had ended. ("Look in the teapot!" was a powerful incantation, the inspired solution to a hundred minor financial crises.) I knew that chucking out all of my mother's perfumes and cosmetics would be bracing; I was unprepared for the way the little green bottle of plant food would refuse to go quietly. There may have been a memorial service and a death certificate to inform the living that Jean Flanagan was gone for good, but the bottle of plant food, mute and loyal as an old dog, was patiently waiting for her return.

My father was a writer with a busy public life. Two librarians from a college in Massachusetts were scheduled to come to the house in a month's time to pack up his papers and manuscripts; an archive was to be established. My mother — war bride, nurse, housewife, imparter of strongly felt political opinions and unsolicited, highly detailed instructions for the preparation of crème caramel and lobster salad, a person to be counted upon in almost any kind of emergency — led the kind of life that is composed of countless acts of service, none of which lend themselves to the creation of a special collection in a college library. A team of archivists was not flying from Massachusetts to find out why she was so often the first person called when there was a disaster (when a friend's son killed himself; when a suspicious lump proved malignant), and also the first to be notified — often by several different friends on the same morning — when Lucky's ran a special on baby asparagus. No one was coming to catalog her recipes or take careful note of the way she organized her spatulas and slotted spoons (all shoved into a glazed pot by the stove, not pretty, but close to hand; useful). The people in charge of dismantling the kitchen were her two daughters: my sister, who had patiently learned all the old lessons, and me, who had spent a childhood planning to be exactly like my mother, but who had somehow failed to pick up the gist of the material. What was I going to take from that kitchen that could catch me up, speed me through a thousand failed tutorials, turn me into someone I should have become years ago?

I opened a kitchen drawer. Its contents were as familiar to me as my children's faces. The bone-handled carving knife, the yellow egg timer, the battered set of aluminum measuring spoons — so useful for doling out baking soda, and also for keeping a hungry baby occupied for a minute or two while a bottle of milk warms in a bath of hot water. I had no practical need for any of the things in that drawer. I own a fancy set of Williams-Sonoma retractable measuring spoons; I have a Gerber carving knife in a velvet-lined case. I rarely use either of them. What I needed from that kitchen wasn't any practical thing, so what I took were the three least practical things I could find: a tiny gadget made for slicing green beans — one at a time — into juliennes, an old Mouli parsley grater, a Pyrex measuring cup so old that the red lines indicating measurement had worn off. I took them as souvenirs. I took them to say: someone noticed.

• • •

THIS IS A BOOK about the things that have always interested me the most: women and children, households and marriages. It is the story of an age told not on battlefields or in courtrooms, but in the places women love and loathe: laundry rooms and nurseries, sunny kitchens and dark ones, the marriage bed. It's a book grounded in my fascination with the old routines and rhythms of orderly housekeeping, and in my equally strong suspicion of those routines, my fear that devotion to them is a trap, capable of snaring my ambition and worldly talent. I began writing it shortly after my mother died, when I was just beginning to realize that her life — lived though it was in the shadow of someone with a successful career — may have been not only the more worthwhile, but perhaps also the more rewarding.

The book was also born from my own experiences as a wife and mother, and from a series of assignments on family life that I was given by two national magazines. As I wrote about housekeeping and marriage and motherhood, I was engaged in an extensive practicum on the subjects. The assignments colored my daily round with an agreeable measure of academic inquiry. I wrote an essay on the anticlutter movement two weeks after Christmas, when my house was filled to the gunwales with stuff and I was being driven mad by it. I wrote about the contradictions and casual brutalities of the current nanny culture after coming to terms with my own role in that culture. Once my editor called me and said that he believed there was an epidemic of sexless marriages in America, and I told him he was wrong. Two weeks later three people in a row confessed they were living in one, or knew someone who was, and so I wrote about that, too.

Over and over I found myself writing about a paradox that became more obvious with each assignment I took: as women have achieved ever more power in the world — power of a kind my mother and her friends from nursing school could never have imagined — they have become increasingly attracted to the privileges and niceties of traditional womanhood. Because they buck the obligations and restraints that gave those privileges meaning, they have become obsessed with a drag queen ethos, in which femininity must be communicated by exaggeration and cartoon.

The elaborate white wedding made an astonishing comeback when hardened career girls in their mid-thirties suddenly wanted to don virginal white gowns and have their fathers transfer them to their grooms in front of flower-decked altars. Celebrity homemakers — including Martha Stewart as high priestess — proved that a successful, liberated woman could care deeply, meaningfully, spiritually about the precise state of her linen closet. Modern wives, many of whom enjoyed premarital sex lives of notable friskiness, suddenly adopted the "not tonight dear" approach to sexuality of the nineteen-fifties housewife.

About motherhood there is the deepest conflict of all. Affluent working mothers stubbornly insist that no one question their commitment to their children, while at-home mothers demand that the world confer on them the social cachet that comes with working outside the home. But these are mutually exclusive demands.

What few will admit — because it is painful, because it reveals the unpleasant truth that life presents a series of choices, each of which precludes a host of other attractive possibilities — is that whichever decision a woman makes, she will lose something of incalculable value. The kind of relationship formed between a child and a mother who is home all day caring for him is substantively different from that formed between a child and a woman who is gone many hours a week. The former relationship is more intimate, more private, filled with more moments of maternal frustration — and even despair — and with more moments of the transcendence that comes only from mothering a small child.

Yet when a woman works outside the home, she uses the best of her mind and education, exerting her authority and power on the world beyond her doorstep. We respect women who stay home with their children, but it's the ones who work — the ones who spend their days taking part in the commerce and traffic of the adult world — who seem to have retained the most of their former selves.

That many women have to work because of financial necessity often precludes serious discussion of these issues. What could be more heartless than highlighting the emotional losses posed to mother and child by their separation because of maternal employment? Yet in writing this book I decided not to skirt the question of what happens to the relationship between mother and child when they are separated, for long hours, because of work. Unpopular though the subject may be, the book would be dishonest if I didn't confront it, in full and without apology, so that's what I've done.

●   ●   ●

I WAS BORN in 1961, which I believe makes me a member of the very last generation of American women born before feminism began to redefine the parameters and expectations of a healthy girlhood. When I was a child, it was understood that girls would evince a natural interest in homemaking, and it was believed that such interest was to be encouraged. It was also understood that we would have a keen interest in establishing a romantic life, and that these two interests — in households and husbands — would emerge early in our lives and would eventually dovetail one another perfectly. By second grade I had white go-go boots and a plan to marry Paul McCartney, nineteen years my senior, but these things could be worked out. I had an Easy-Bake Oven and my mother's old alligator pumps and a complete set of the Laura Ingalls Wilder books and a miniature Hoover vacuum cleaner, which made a tiny roar when you ran it. I was ready for anything.

While I was growing up, I was aware that off to the side — mixed up with adult things like the Vietnam war and cocktails — there was something called women's lib and after that there was something called the women's movement, and the mothers in our circle seemed very worked up about these things. To these two forces I owe any number of the rights I take for granted, such as my ability to establish credit in my own name, apply for a business loan, pilot an airplane, get an abortion, work construction, and sue the bejesus out of a male coworker who gooses me in the coffee room. I've never had the occasion or the desire to do any of these things, but if the moment strikes, the way has been made straight for me.

But this is not a book about equal rights or equal opportunities. It is a book about what came after those things had been secured. It is about what conservatives call the feminist agenda and what I call the new prescription for female unhappiness. It's about the notion that caring for children and husbands and households constitutes subservience, and the notion that girls should be pushed toward competition and professional life rather than homemaking. It is about the stubborn longing for an earlier way of life, and about the way that longing manifests and reasserts itself in the imagination of so many modern women. It is less a book about what we have gained than it is a book about what we have lost, and if there is something of the elegy in it, so be it. For those who may be distressed by the ideas herein, there is infinite solace: it is only a book about a ruined city. When I was writing it — when I was thinking about my own girlhood, and when I was stunned with grief over the loss of my mother — I had some words from a Davison Jeffers poem taped up on the refrigerator door. Here they are:

There is no reason for amazement; surely one always knew that cultures decay, and life's end is death.

To Hell with All That

The Virgin Bride

I DO NOT PLAN to have another wedding; I'm standing pat at two. But I must confess that after spending a pleasant hour gazing at the photographs in a recent crop of wedding guides, I began to feel a bit of the old itch. There is something deeply seductive about a wedding: romance in its great last stand, not yet sullied by routine and responsibility. Even a photograph of that ill-fated girl Diana Spencer, standing on the steps of St. Paul's, her veil caught in a gust of wind and her father waiting to take her hand, can provoke in me a vague yet undeniable longing. But it took only a few minutes of actually reading the texts of these manuals to bring me to my senses. More

3

than fondness for my husband keeps me from getting on the phone to price tea roses and a tent.

Planning a wedding is hell. Things are said. Doors are slammed. Quarrels about the most inconsequential things — yellow tablecloths or white? hors d'oeuvres set out on tables or passed around on trays? — are often pitched at such a level that it seems the combatants may never recover from them. Much of the anxiety, of course, is tribal. It is wrenching to have to open the sacred circle to admit an outsider. If, as Joan Didion once wrote, "marriage is the classic betrayal," a wedding is the Judas kiss, public and terrible. But what brings people almost to the breaking point (emotional, social, financial) is that white weddings as they are currently practiced in America — with flocks of attendants, dinner dances for hundreds of guests, and a code governing every moment of the proceedings — don't come naturally to most. Perhaps they don't come naturally to anybody other than the members of the $70-billion-a-year wedding industry, who seem to have all but created the contemporary event, weaving together attractive bits of genuine tradition and bolts of pure invention.

Before World War II the idea that a girl of modest means would expect any of today's purchased grandeur would have been laughable. She would have been familiar with the elements of such a ceremony, would have seen lavish movie weddings and photographs of society and royal ones, but she would not have imagined that those events had much to do with her own plans. She would have been married much as her mother had been: with her best friend standing up for her and everyone looking forward to a nice party at the bride's home, the two mothers wearing corsages and ladling punch.

But times have changed, and middle-class couples are routinely trading the down payment on a first house for a single eye-popping party. Ilene Beckerman ponders the shift in the charming little book *Mother of the Bride: The Dream, the Reality, the Search for a Perfect Dress.* After being confronted with her daughter's hideously complex reception menu, Beckerman can't help herself: "When your father and I were married at your grandmother's house in Queens," she tells her aggrieved daughter, "we served deli platters. Everybody loved them."

Nowadays every aspect of a formal wedding has become so intensely merchandized as to render its original design and purpose almost unrecognizable. The bridal registry, for example, was once a means by which a young couple could acquire the basic accoutrements of good house-keeping. Now couples old enough to have fully stocked homes — not to mention full-grown children — register for loot. They can be seen trolling through Williams-Sonoma, Pottery Barn, and Target, carrying bar code scanners and zapping anything that looks good. The trend toward multiple showers means that a guest may return to a couple's registry several times. Web sites such as WeddingChannel.com and The Knot provide an opportunity for couples to showcase their weddings for their friends — and to put those friends a click away from the bride's registry, where a gift can be selected and paid for in a matter of minutes.

Everything is big. The wedding invitation, once the model of a certain kind of brevity, is now often a mere component of a thick dossier with multiple stamps. "What's this fat, unsolicited envelope in your mail, packed with forms that you must fill out and instructions that you must obey?" asks Judith Martin in her *Miss Manners on Weddings*. She concludes that it is, in fact, a wedding invitation from "people who have gone around the bend." In the many published accounts of people's experiences planning and hosting weddings, couples are constantly getting blindsided by the professionals, never imagining the pressure that vendors would put on them to consider various trifles absolutely essential. Just as the morticians whom Jessica Mitford described in *The American Way of Death* preyed on the grief and guilt of mourners, so do the wedding merchants capitalize on the emotional vulnerability and social anxiety that afflict people planning a formal wedding. If you love her, shouldn't you spend two months' salary on the diamond she's going to wear forever? Would you deny a cherished daughter the same sort of party that all her friends have had?

In a memoir detailing her engagement, wedding, and early married life, *Something New: Reflections on the Beginnings of a Marriage,* Amanda Beesley describes a moment of clarity in which the economics of her planned event came into sharp focus: she had spent a month's rent on her dress, and "the 'deluxe' Porta-Johns, with mirrors and running water," that she had selected "would have paid off two months' worth of my student loan." Setting aside the advisability of buying an expensive dress for anything that is going to involve Porta-Johns, no matter how whiz-bang, the confession is hardly unusual: young people routinely engineer weddings that are well beyond their means.

How did we get here? The idea that the formal white wedding might not be within the purview solely of society types began during the postwar rush to the altar, which saw droves of working people — who finally had a bit of money in their pockets — having weddings more elaborate than their parents'. The first American book devoted to bridal etiquette was published in 1948, heralding the notion that one might clip from an entire volume of social convention a single attractive chapter.

The hugely influential 1950 movie *Father of the Bride* traded on the new national interest in the particulars of this kind of event, and it portrayed the shift toward grander weddings. Although the bride's parents are well-off, they were married simply, "in your front parlor," Mr. Banks reminds his wife. She is unmoved by this memory or by her husband's pride in having worn a plain blue suit rather than a cutaway. Despite the old man's remonstrations, it is decided that their daughter, iconically played by Elizabeth Taylor, will not follow this family tradition. She will have a different kind of wedding, "with bridesmaids and churches and automobiles and flowers and all that." (Although the film's wedding provided a specific fantasy for a generation of young women, many of today's brides would turn up their noses at it. Refreshments consisted of finger sandwiches, ice cream, and tea cakes.) Facilitating the new preference for such affairs was the growing availability in the fifties of both mass-produced wedding gowns and rented formal wear for men. This kind of institutionalized formality, however, had a difficult time coexisting with the social upheaval of the sixties, and by the seventies the big white wedding (along with its dud pal, marriage) was in a period of retrenchment. Tricia Nixon's 1971 wedding in the Rose Garden was considered by many to be Squaresville itself.

The lights came back on in the summer of 1981, when alarm clocks rang in the dead of night so that millions of Americans could witness Charles and Diana plighting their troth in real time. The doings of the British royal family may constitute a poor template for contemporary American life, but the timing was right. The Reagans had just begun their stylish reign, and lavish entertaining had made a triumphant return. The wedding world changed and has stayed changed.

The problem is that we put the formal white wedding into cold storage for so long that we're a little unclear about what, exactly, is involved. Further, the social changes that have so profoundly reshaped American life in the past half century have mowed down virtually every institution that the traditional wedding once sanctified. To stage a white wedding as the form was originally conceived requires a woman young enough that her very age suggests a measure of innocence, the still-married parents who have harbored her up to this point, and a young man of like religious affiliation who is willing to assume responsibility for her keep. Trying to pull off this piece of theater in light of the divorce culture, the women's movement, the sexual revolution, and the acceptability of mixed and later marriages threatens to make a complete mockery of the thing. It's like trying to stage a nativity pageant without a baby and a donkey: you can do it, but you're going to need one hell of a manger.

The modern bride, of course, doesn't dwell on any of this. She is, after all, the daughter of one of the most profound cultural shifts in American history, and this is part of her birthright: the freedom to sample, on an à la carte basis, the various liberties that young womanhood offers.

She can gratefully accept a handful of condoms from her guidance counselor and also be assured that no one will laugh when she shows up at her wedding, on her father's arm, wearing a floor-length beaded white gown. And besides, there's no *time* to think about all this — there's so much to *do!* Sending welcome baskets to the hotel rooms of out-of-town guests, learning the precise way to tether a gold band to the ring bearer's satin pillow, discerning which participants must be thanked not only with a note but also with a gift — there's no end to it.

Fortunately, in view of this bewildering array of wedding essentials, a standing army of professionals has been quietly assembled during the past two decades, one consisting of salespeople and "wedding coordinators" and Web site designers and also authors who have flooded the market with wedding books so numerous that they would force the library at Alexandria to resort to auxiliary storage. Most of the books fall roughly into three categories: etiquette books that attempt to pistol-whip the masses into decent behavior; glossy wish books that hope to imbue the readers' events with the authors' own good taste; and gritty down-and-dirties that address the awfulness of it all head-on, albeit comically.

A faction of renegade brides realizes that the wedding business is a racket and rejects the notion of busting the bank for one 5-hour party. The problem occurs when they try to procure bargain-basement opulence, to cut corners ruthlessly on a fancy party rather than throw a simpler one. The suggestion offered by a bargain wedding expert that one might offer a full bar but issue each guest two drink tickets is just a bad, bad idea. I encountered a description of a Vera Wang sample sale that made the event sound like a little corner of hell, with punchy, exhausted brides waiting in line for hours in hopes of scoring a bit of picked-over cut-rate couture.

It's hard to get it right when it comes to this particular intersection of money and class. No less an authority than *Weddings for Dummies* sums up the problem nicely — or, rather, Epictetus does: "Know, first, who you are; and then adorn yourself accordingly." Leave it to one of the ancients to put a fine point on a modern problem: weddings today are often made comical or ghastly by their obvious overtones of strenuous social climbing. The editor in chief of *Brides* magazine, Millie Martini Bratten, told me that the modern wedding represents "a chance to reach beyond your station," and she's right. Class aspiration is nothing new, but there was certainly a time when a girl who aped the ways of rich folk on her wedding day would have won herself more derision than respect.

The wedding merchants know that selling "class" would set off alarms in most people's heads, so what they proffer instead is "tradition," and the modern bride pays cash on the barrelhead for it, never realizing that the wholesale acquisition of other people's traditions is an enterprise fraught with pitfalls. (If she put down *Legendary Brides* for a minute and picked up *The Great Gatsby* instead, she might think twice.)

Genuine tradition is not for sale, because no one needs to buy it; it's moored in the customs of one's own family (remember them?). If Dad feels like a complete chump in his Sir Elegance tux, you've just learned something about your tradition. What the altar-bound of today end up buying from their numberless vendors is a dog's breakfast of bridal excess — part society wedding of the twenties, part Long Island Italian wedding of the fifties. It's *The Philadelphia Story* and *The Wedding Singer* served up together in one curious and costly buffet.

When the etiquette experts are asked about these hybrid events, how can they possibly know to which standards the questioner is hoping to hew? Often couples want to throw weddings that will be interpreted as "social" (WASP classy) but that include whatever "ethnic" elements look good to them. Miss Manners, by her own admission, tends "to become snappish during wedding season," and I don't blame her. When she attempts to construct a firebreak, she gets blasted. She informed one mother of the bride that her daughter's plan to carry a "money bag" with her during the reception constituted nothing less than "simple social blackmail." "She is counting on the guests forking over under the threat of embarrassment. This is not exactly what we call hospitality." But another

Gentle Reader scolded Miss Manners for failing to do some research on other cultures in which such a custom is commonplace: "If Miss Manners thinks her uppity manners prevail everywhere, she has another think coming." Emily Post — now in the guise of her great-granddaughter-in-law Peggy Post, in *Emily Post's Wedding Etiquette* — deals with ethnic variances by abandoning her station and going PC. Peggy lumps the lucrative customs — including the "money dance," which, if successfully completed, results in "bride and groom . . . covered with cash" — together with central elements of Jewish and traditional African American weddings in a separate chapter called (you guessed it) "Multicultural Weddings."

Bridal salespeople toss around the words *tradition* and *heirloom* with a galling vulgarity that is particularly evident in a captivating Learning Channel series called *A Wedding Story*. Each episode of the documentary-style program follows one couple through their courtship and engagement (as recounted during crosscut interviews with bride and groom), and the cameras tag along to the rehearsal, the ceremony, and the reception. The couples often have solid but not especially high-paying jobs (*Wedding Story* careers have included hairstylist, nurse, and police officer); they spend what must be a staggering portion of their incomes on these events, and they can often be glimpsed at the very point of purchase.

In one episode an engaged couple, Ivette and Joe, are

led into a jeweler's inner sanctum to get a first look at the ring they have ordered. But as the salesman relinquishes it to them for inspection, he rattles off a bit of boilerplate: "This is the beginning of your family's heirloom. This is what you're going to pass on to your children and your children's children. It is the thing that bonds the two of you, and I want you to appreciate it and treat it that way." Ivette and Joe do not seem at all surprised to find themselves lectured to by a diamond merchant. In our culture the wise counselors who instruct young people on the most important ritual of their lives *are* salesmen. Nor do the couple seem to realize that if the man is telling the truth, they can simply go home empty-handed and wait for a family member to fork over *Ivette's* heirloom ring.

One opulent wedding guide, *Weddings: A Celebration,* by Beverly Clark, lionizes the gimmick of a bride who bought a seventeenth-century Bible in which couples — presumably of the same family — had recorded important events for some three hundred years. She and her groom then added their wedding date to the list, a gesture of almost comical crassness. A family tradition, it turns out, is something that fancy folk do and that you can do, too — against the knowledge that your future daughter may not have any more truck with your choices than you had with your mother's.

Of course, the woman who long ago branded tradition as a commodity on the American open market is Martha

Stewart, and she established a beachhead in the wedding business early on. With her uncanny ability to predict — and often to forge — the hottest societal trends, she was on top of the white-wedding craze not long after Princess Diana braced herself and thought of England. Stewart's 1987 publishing phenomenon, *Weddings,* helped to cement her reputation as one of our most important cultural figures. Its pride of place in the wedding-wish-book canon has been challenged only by the publication of a second volume, *The Best of Martha Stewart Living: Weddings.*

In fairness, Stewart has always been great at fanning the mini-flames of actual tradition. In the introduction to her first book, *Entertaining,* she wrote that when she wants the "comfort of childhood" to come flooding back, she whips up some of her mother's Polish specialties, some nice "pierogi or stuffed cabbage." One has long sensed, however, that it is other people's traditions that she really has her eye on, and the autobiographical sketch in *Weddings* gives a clue as to whose traditions they are. When she decided to marry Andy Stewart, "it seemed appropriate to be married in St. Paul's Chapel at Columbia in an Episcopalian service, mainly because we didn't have anyplace else to go." It sounds like a lovely affair, but surely it would have been "appropriate," strictly speaking, for an *Episcopalian* (or — talk about "appropriate" — two of them) to be married in St. Paul's Chapel at Columbia in an Episcopal service.

The Stewart enterprise is powerful enough and thoroughly enough girded with her unquestionable style (my God, the woman's way with simple white daisies) that many absurdities get subsumed in the larger picture. The irony is that many Stewart-inspired events are occasions from which members of the true WASP ascendancy — frugal, abhorrent of excess — would flee as fast as their skinny little legs could carry them. The WASPs whom the wedding merchants hope to conjure are more on the order of the robber barons and their families — people like Alva Vanderbilt, who managed to fuse her daughter Consuelo to the Duke of Marlborough and celebrated the family's new acquisition in an explosion of pink and white flowers in St. Thomas Episcopal Church on Fifth Avenue. Or they're WASPs as imagined by Hollywood screenwriters: Katharine Hepburn's Tracy Lord invited 506 guests to the reception after her second wedding in *The Philadelphia Story.* Couples who think they are striking a classically American chord with their tuxedo-clad swing bands and galaxies of trumpet lilies might consider the sentiments of the super-WASP poet Elinor Wylie (who left her husband for a married man — no wonder we look to these people for wedding day guidance): "Down to the Puritan marrow of my bones / There's something in this richness that I hate."

If class confusion is the order of the day at many white weddings, these occasions are also chock-full of conflicting messages regarding the bride's sexual experience. The white dress; the handoff from father to groom; the lifting of the veil, which undresses the bride just a bit; and the presence of flowers and small children (evoking the fertility that will soon be unleashed) are all popular components — in various combinations — of the modern wedding.

Perhaps most representative of this ambiguity is the kiss that concludes the wedding ceremony, permission for which is granted only after bride and groom have been legally transformed into man and wife. Often, Miss Manners writes, the kiss "draws laughter, as if it were a love scene viewed by an audience of early adolescents." Although few couples would forgo this crowd-pleasing bit of business, many have reshaped its purpose, using it not to mark a newly sanctioned physical relationship but rather to give a peek at one that is already red-hot. More than once during the rehearsals on *A Wedding Story*, I have seen the officiant instruct the intendeds to approach this moment with a bit of decorum. What patsies these poor clergy members must feel like, forced into the role of a sexual naif primly instructing a young man who has been living with his girlfriend for the past three years that he "may kiss the bride." Well, why not? He's been doing God knows what else to her since the night they met at the softball league happy hour.

To pick up an issue of *Brides* magazine, which has been instructing American women on weddings since

1934, is to find this confusion writ large. In one respect *Brides* harks back to a time when women's magazines never mentioned sex at all and the advice on offer was of a most genteel nature. A recent issue is full of the kind of pointers that well-bred mothers have given their daughters for generations: write the thank-you note as soon as you get the gift; send the announcement to the newspaper several weeks before the wedding. The advertisements (and they are staggering in number) feature brides so demure that many of them can't even look us in the eye; they gaze off in deepest repose or trail clouds of tulle through the marble lobby of the Ritz-Carlton, Pentagon City. The reader of *Brides,* it seems, is meant to make an imaginative leap, to enter a world of untouched ladies preparing chastely for their most special day.

And yet. I'm not quite sure what to make of the young miss who writes that "a few months ago, my fiancé and I" — "fiancé": old-fashioned word, isn't it? — "started watching porn together," which has caused the couple a specific problem that I had no idea was within the purview of *Brides* magazine. Then there's the unfortunate woman who seems to have spent down her sexual capital a little too early in the game: "I promised my fiancé that once we were engaged, I'd do anything he wanted, sexually speaking. Now he's suggesting a threesome." (This is one of the reasons those unliberated but canny girls of an earlier era didn't put out until after they had tossed the bouquet:

they didn't want to have to put the kibosh on icky sexual fantasies before they'd established joint checking.)

The problem of introducing drama to the wedding night is a big one, and *Brides* tackles it unflinchingly. It's uphill all the way. The bride should consider packing her honeymoon suitcase with "a bunch of sex-research books" and "two highlighter pens in two different colors." Call Domino's and pass the No-Doz; it's gonna be an all-nighter. If she's absolutely determined to unveil a new trick, the bride might consider a suggestion that involves a thirty-six-inch strand of acrylic pearls, preferably strung on nylon, and some water-based personal lubricant, although she is cautioned (in what may be the issue's single best piece of advice) to "be careful with the necklace's clasp."

In one sense all this is in line with the kind of information to be found in many magazines aimed at today's young single women — publications that have supplemented frank information about reproductive health with step-by-step sexual instruction. (A typical copy of *Jane* makes the Kama Sutra look like a compendium of calisthenics for senior citizens.) It seems in today's climate that only prudes and religious fanatics suggest that young women ought to forgo sexual experience before marriage. Very few grooms, certainly, are troubled by a bride's colorful past. *Marry Me!* is a book by three "professional guys" who share the secrets of snaring one of their elite confraternity (and any woman hell-bent on becoming the helpmeet of an orthopedic surgeon, an accountant, or a lawyer should by all means pony up the $13.98 for Amazon's overnight-shipping option). Along with some repeated — and to my mind rather pointed — advice along the lines of "*Never comment in any way about your man's penis being small*" (italics not my own), the brain trust informs readers how many men they can sleep with and still end up married to a CPA: ten. You're not necessarily out of luck if you worked your way through most of Sigma Chi during junior year, but you are going to have to lie about it.

But the sexual experience (or, rather, sexual ennui) of the contemporary couple accounts in no small part for why — much to the delight of caterers and banquet hall operators everywhere — today's wedding receptions seem never to end. With only a dispiriting and possibly dangerous interlude with acrylic pearls awaiting them in the bridal suite, there is nothing to hurry the principals off the dance floor. The couple are far more interested in boogying down at the opulent party they've ordered — after all the hard work, a chance to have some fun! — than in attending to the drudgery of consummating the marriage. There was a time when a wedding wasn't just a fancy party, when it commemorated an occasion of tremendous moment, as true ritual always has — in this case the beginning of a woman's sexual life. The reception was once marked by a particular kind of shared anxiety, which fostered a genre of American humor that is now all but lost: the wedding night joke. The clanging of tin cans tied to getaway cars struck a primal note that nobody failed to locate and that no amount of Ritz-Carlton catering can ever reproduce.

Today a wedding unites a couple who may or may not spend the rest of their lives together and who may or may not have nullified the spirit of their every promise with an ironclad prenuptial agreement. Usually the sexual union has already occurred, and oftentimes cohabitation, with its disappointments and indignities, is in full swing. A bride's beautiful white gown and her flock of flower-bearing attendants may constitute nothing more than an enduring female attraction to the sort of thing that would make Betty Friedan lean her old gray head against the keyboard and weep. Or they may be part of a frantic and terribly expensive effort to infuse a wedding with some small measure of the meaning it once had.

Nearly forty years ago, Joan Didion reported, in *Slouching Towards Bethlehem,* on the Las Vegas wedding industry — which, she found, was *not* based solely on "the premise that marriage, like craps, is a game to be played when the table seems hot." She found instead that the Vegas wedding chapels, "with their wishing wells and stained-glass paper windows and their artificial bouvardia," were in fact selling "'niceness,' the facsimile of proper ritual, to children who do not know how else to find it."

Today's children do know where to find "proper ritual." They find it in a thousand showrooms and expos and trunk sales; they skip out on student loans to pay for it; and when they need more cash for the limos, they transform their bridal registries into complicated money-laundering operations (a place setting of Lenox is, after all, a liquid asset). One can't help thinking that they would trade every bit of it for one simple, elusive assurance: only death will part us.

The Wifely Duty

NOT LONG AGO, during two strange days in New York, three married people — one after another — confessed to me either that they had stopped having sex or that they knew a married person who had stopped having sex. Like a sensible person, I booked an early flight home and chalked the whole thing up to the magic and mystery that is New York. But no sooner had I put my coat on the peg than it started up again. A number of the mothers in my set began making sardonic comments along similar lines. The daytime talk shows to which I am mildly and happily addicted worried the subject to death, revived it, and worried it some more. Dr. Phil — who, like his mentor Oprah Winfrey, has an uncannily precise sense of what American women in the aggregate are fretting about — noted on his Web site that "sexless marriages are an undeniable epidemic." Mass-circulation magazines aimed at married women rarely go to press these days without an earnest review of some new sexual technique or gadget, the information always presented in the context of how to relight a long-doused fire. (And I must say that an article in *Redbook* that warns desperate couples away from a product called Good Head Oral Delight Gel — "the consistency is like congealed turkey fat" — deserves some kind of award for service journalism.) Patricia Heaton, for many years a star of *Everybody Loves Raymond*, has observed, "Sex? Forget about it. I mean that literally." Books with titles such as *Okay, So I Don't Have a Headache* and *I'm Not in the Mood* have become immediate hits, and another popular book, *For Women Only*, lists various techniques that married women use to avoid sex, from the age-old strategy of feigning sleep to the quite modern practice of taking on household night owl projects. And Allison Pearson's much-loved novel about a busy working mother, *I Don't Know How She Does It* (which opens with the main character engaged in just such a late-night project), features a woman so tired that she's frantic to escape sex with her husband, prompting Margaret Carlson, of *Time* magazine, to remark, "Sleep is the new sex." It has become impossible not to suspect that a large number of relatively young and otherwise healthy married people are forgoing sex for long periods of time and that many have given it up altogether.

And so we turn our curious attention to the marital therapist Michele Weiner Davis, whose 2003 book *The Sex-Starved Marriage* is certain to puzzle generations of social historians. The book is not particularly interested in the cause of this strange turn of events, although Davis tosses around the expected observations about the exhaustion that dogs contemporary working parents and the reduction in lust that has always gone along with marriage. Hers is not a deep-thinking, reflective kind of book, but, rather, a get-cracking-and-solve-the-problem kind of book. Solutions? She's armed to the teeth with them. She has created a "passion-building toolkit" filled with "field-tested" techniques — none of them bad. Although I found Part IV ("Doing It Together") far more appealing than a scary mini-chapter called "The Do-It-Yourself Solution," her notions about how to jump-start the old hanky-panky seem eminently reasonable. Make "romantic overtures," she counsels. A wife might buy some new lingerie; a husband might wear flattering clothes.

Most important, though, is a recommendation based on exciting new "research" revealing that for many people, waiting for the urge to strike is pointless; better to bash ahead and hope for the best. Davis asks, "Have you ever noticed that although you might not have been thinking sexual thoughts or feeling particularly sexy, if you push yourself to 'get started' when your spouse approaches you, it feels good, and you find yourself getting into it?" Many of her clients have received this counsel with enthusiasm. "I really wasn't in the mood for sex at all," reports one of her advisees after just such a night, "but once we got started, it was fun. I really enjoyed it."

What's odd here is not the suggestions themselves — each seems quite sensible, and I myself can vouch for more than one of them — but, rather, the generation that apparently needs them. American adults under the age of fifty tend to know more about sex and its many delightful permutations than did streetwalkers of an earlier century. When Davis describes the process of arousal ("You notice a feeling of fullness in your pelvic area as your genitals become engorged with blood"), you might think she was addressing a seventh-grade health class rather than adults of the post–sexual revolution era. Yuppies, with that winsome arrogance that is all their own, proudly describe the nature and frequency of their premarital couplings with a specificity matched only by advanced seminars on animal husbandry. The reason abortion rights hold such a sanctified position in American political life is that they are a critical component of the yuppie program for maximum personal sexual pleasure. But let these inebriates of nooky enter marriage, a state in which ongoing sexuality often has as much to do with old-fashioned notions of obligation and commitment as it does with the immediate satisfaction of intense physical desire, and they grow as cool and limp as yesterday's Cobb salad.

All of this makes me reflect that those repressed and much-pitied fifties wives — their sexless college years! their boorish husbands, who couldn't locate the clitoris with a flashlight and a copy of *Gray's Anatomy*! — were apparently getting a lot more action than many of today's most liberated and sexually experienced married women. In the old days, of course, there was the wifely duty. A housewife understood that in addition to ironing her husband's shirts and cooking the Sunday roast, she was, with some regularity, going to have relations with the man of the house. Perhaps, as some feminists would have us believe, these were grimly efficient interludes during which the poor humped-upon wife stared at the ceiling and silently composed the grocery list. Or perhaps not. Maybe, as Davis and her "new" findings suggest, once you get the canoe out in the water, everybody starts happily paddling. The notion that female sexuality was unleashed forty years ago, after lying dormant lo these uncountable millennia, is silly. More recent is the sexual shutdown that apparently takes place in many marriages soon after they have been legalized.

Jane Greer, *Redbook*'s online sex therapist, has a thriving midtown Manhattan practice. When I asked her about what I had been hearing, she told me that she has seen many married couples who have gone without sex for periods of time ranging from six months to six years. Why? "Marriage has changed," she told me. "In the old days the husband was the breadwinner. The wife had the expectation of raising the children and pleasing him. Now they're both working and both taking care of the children, and they're too exhausted and resentful to have sex." I asked Greer the obvious question: if a couple are not having sex because of job pressures and one partner quits working, does the couple have more sex? The answer was immediate and unequivocal: *"Absolutely!"*

And this, of course, is the general plot of *I Don't Know How She Does It,* which has the heroine, Kate Reddy, playing dead in the sack for a world of nights until, at book's end, she resigns from her job and runs into her husband's arms. "The hug wasn't that dry click of bones you get holding someone when the passion has drained away. It was more like a shadow dance: I still wanted him and I think he wanted me, but we hadn't touched in a very long time." When Kate and her husband reconnect in a London coffee shop after a brief, miserable separation, "we both laugh, and for a moment Starbucks is filled with the sound of Us." (Funny, I thought that grating, deafening sound was the coffee grinder.) Still, though, the book has struck a chord. In an episode of *The Oprah Winfrey Show* devoted to the book, Oprah introduced it as "the new bible for working mothers." In particular, droves of readers report that the nature of Kate's marriage mirrors theirs exactly.

The dominant feature of Kate's attitude toward her husband — that is, before they resume making the sound of Us — is blistering contempt. Contempt for his work: he is a quietly successful architect, given to building whimsical little structures like Peace Pagodas, a pursuit that leaves him time to make pesto and watch Disney videos with the kids while she strides off to her high-paying, high-pressure job. Contempt for his inability to notice when the family has run out of toilet paper or whether the children are properly dressed for a birthday party. Contempt for his very existence in the household: when he wonders whether it would be such a bad thing if their uncooperative nanny quit, Kate tells him, "Frankly, it would be easier if you left." That the man entertains even a single amorous notion about this ballbreaker — much given to kittenish, come-hither comments along the lines of "Richard, I thought I asked you to tidy up?" and "Why the hell can't you do something that needs doing?" — is testament either to a libido of iron or to an erotic sensibility that leans toward the deeply masochistic. If best-selling novels succeed because they "tap into" something in the culture, surely this woman's helpless anger at the man who she thought was going to share her domestic burden accounts in part for the book's immense popularity.

Pearson told an interviewer, "Until they program men to notice you're out of toilet paper, a happy domestic life will always be up to women" — a sentiment almost unanimously held by the working mothers I know. What we've learned during this thirty-year grand experiment is that men can be cajoled into doing all sorts of household tasks, but they will not do them the way a woman would. They will bathe the children, but they will not straighten the bath mat and wring out the washcloths. They will drop a toddler off at nursery school, but they won't spend ten minutes chatting with the teacher and collecting the art projects. They will, in other words, do what men have always done: reduce a job to its simplest essentials and utterly ignore the fillips and niceties that women tend to regard as equally essential. And a lot of women feel cheated and angry and even — bless their hearts — surprised about this.

In the old days, of course, men's inability to perform women's work competently was a source of satisfaction and pride to countless housewives. A reliable sitcom premise involved Father's staying home for a day while Mother handled things at his office; chastened and newly admiring of the other's abilities, each ran gratefully back to familiar terrain. Nowadays, when a working mother arrives home after a late deposition, only to find the living room strewn with Legos and a pizza box crammed into the kitchen trash, she tends to get madder than a wet hen.

Women are left with two options: endlessly haranguing their husbands to be more womanly, or silently fuming and (however wittingly) launching a sex strike of an intensity and a duration that would have impressed Aristophanes. The men who cave to the pressure to become more feminine — putting little notes in the lunch boxes, sweeping up after snack time, the whole bit — may delight their wives, but they probably don't improve their sex lives much, owing to the thorny old problem of *la différence*. I might be quietly thrilled if my husband decided to forgo his weekly tennis game so that he could alphabetize the spices and scrub the lazy Susan, but I would hardly consider it an erotic gesture.

It turns out that the "traditional" marriage, which we've all been so happy to annihilate, had some pretty good provisions for many of today's most stubborn marital problems, such as how to combine work and parenthood, and how to keep the springs of the marriage bed in good working order. What's interesting about the sex advice given to married women of earlier generations is that it proceeds from the assumption that in a marriage a happy sex life depends upon orderly and successful housekeeping.

Marabel Morgan's notorious 1973 book *The Total Woman* has lingered in people's minds because of the seduction techniques it recommends to unhappy housewives. They ought to consider meeting their husbands at the front door in sexy costumes (heels and lingerie, that kind of thing), calling them at work and talking dirty to them, seducing them beneath the dining room table. (Morgan does not, however, recommend that women nurture a burning intelligence. In a list of unconventional locations in which to make love, she includes the hammock, counseling her readers, "He may say 'We don't have a hammock.' You can reply 'Oh, darling, I forgot!'") But long before she describes any of these memorable techniques, Morgan gives a quite thorough accounting of how a housewife ought to go about "redeeming the time" and the energy so that she is physically and emotionally able to make love on a regular basis. A housewife should run her household the way an executive runs his business: with goals, schedules, and plans. She should make dinner — or at least do all the shopping and planning for it — right after breakfast, so that she isn't running around like a madwoman in the late afternoon with no idea what to cook. She should take time to rest and relax during the day so that she is not exhausted and depleted come whoopee hour. With the right kind of planning, "you can have all your home duties finished before noon." In a household run by an incompetent wife, however, "by the time her husband enters the scene, she's had it," Morgan writes. "She's too tired to be available to him." This seems a fairly accurate depiction of many contemporary two-career marriages, in which dinner is a nightly crisis (what to eat?) and an endless negotiation (who to cook it?) entered into by two people who have been managing crises and negotiating agreements all day long and who still have the children's homework and baths and bedtimes to contend with.

A document in circulation on the Internet purports to be a list contained in a fifties home economics book and announces that it is designed to offer future wives "preparation for married life." I recently attended a dinner party at which this list was read aloud by the hostess, to general hilarity, and I know of at least two classrooms (one at a prep school, the other at a graduate school) where it was read and received in similar sidesplitting fashion. The book advises the housewife to prepare for her husband's arrival at the end of the day: to have dinner ready, to minimize household noise and clutter, to avoid assaulting her man with a litany of domestic problems and disappointments, and to inquire about his day. There was a sense back in those innocent years that a day at the office was a tiring event that required a bit of recuperation: a cold drink, a sympathetic companion, a decent meal — all of which, I suspect, functioned as a sexual tonic.

The modern professional workday, as we all know, is far more demanding than its predecessors. It lasts much longer, and the various technologies that were supposed to liberate workers from the office have in fact made the whole world an office. (I recently sat on an otherwise deserted tropical beach, a few minutes after a spectacular sunrise, and watched a middle-aged American man march grimly through pellucid knee-high surf, barking commands on a cell phone.) When a professional person crosses the threshold at the end of the day, the commute hasn't provided a transition from work; it has been a continuation of it, thanks to the array of pagers, phones, and even Internet connections available to the modern driver. And — here's the kicker — there isn't just one spouse who has had such a punishing day; there are two of them. No one has spent even a moment planning a gentle reentry into home life, let alone plotting a thrilling seduction.

Adding to a modern wife's reluctance to seduce the old man on a regular basis is the fact that her job outside the home has conferred on her a power that housewives simply didn't possess. *The Total Woman* assumes that keeping a husband sexually happy is a direct route to a measure of economic power for the wife. A couple of days after Morgan's first night of giving her husband "super sex," he calls her to make sure that she will be home at three o'clock: "I couldn't imagine what was coming and I was stunned to see a truck pull up with a new refrigerator-freezer. . . . Now, without being nagged, he was beginning to give me what I yearned for." Later he lets her redecorate the family room. The women with whom Morgan shares the secrets of super sex (which, in case you are wondering, include not only making dinner early but also moaning a lot during sex and keeping your hands moving on your husband's body throughout intercourse) also get their share of perks. One delighted postcoital woman breathlessly reports to her classmates in a Total Woman workshop, "He has never brought me a gift before, but this past week he bought me two nighties, two rose bushes, and a can opener!" (Ah, would that Dr. Freud were still with us to contemplate that can opener.)

Although I have an amused tolerance for books like *The Total Woman,* I am not entirely incapable of good old-fashioned feminist rage. The notion that even educated middle-class American women had to put out in order to get a damn refrigerator — even that they might "yearn" for one — just steams me. However, I would not advise against using sex for more subtle marital adjustments, of a type described in *The Sex-Starved Marriage.* Davis reminds women that one of the more effective ways to get a husband to be more considerate and helpful is to seduce him. She counsels a group of female clients who complain of angry, critical husbands to "pay more attention to their physical relationships with their husbands," to "be sexier, more affectionate, attentive, responsive, and passionate." Darned if the old bag of tricks doesn't work like a charm: the ladies arrive at the next therapy session giggling and thrilled with their new powers.

To many contemporary women, however, the notion that sex might have any function other than personal fulfillment (and the occasional bit of carefully scheduled baby making) is a violation of the very tenets of the sexual revolution that so deeply shaped their attitudes on such matters. Under these conditions, pity the poor married man hoping to get a bit of comfort from the wife at day's end. He must somehow seduce a woman who is economically independent of him, bone tired, philosophically disinclined to have sex unless she is jolly well in the mood, numbingly familiar with his every sexual maneuver, and still doing a slow burn over his failure to wipe down the countertops and fold the dish towel after cooking the kids' dinner. He can hardly be blamed for opting instead to check his e-mail, catch a few minutes of *SportsCenter*, and call it a night.

A final, less quantifiable development has served to snuff out marital sexuality, and it has to do with the way middle-class and upper-middle-class adults think about family life and their role in it. There are many indications of this, but let us simply glance at the Disney catalogue. Not surprisingly, in addition to toys and figurines the catalogue features Disney-themed clothing: bathrobes with Winnie the Pooh appliqués, stretch knit pants with a small Mickey Mouse at the hem, quilted "Magic Winter Jackets" featuring a choice of Eeyore, Mickey, or Pooh. Here's the problem: all these items are for adults. In fact, I was horrified to discover that it would have been possible for my husband and me to spend last Halloween trick-or-treating in matching Tweedledum and Tweedledee costumes —

a pretty far cry from Marabel Morgan's idea of a good costume.

For many couples child rearing has become not merely one aspect of marriage, but its entire purpose and function. Spouses regard each other principally not as lovers and companions, but as sharers of the great, unending burden of taking care of the children. And make no mistake about it: American middle-class families have made child rearing a dauntingly complex enterprise. When my children were still very small, it was made abundantly clear to me by friends and acquaintances that I had better get in the market for an SUV or a minivan, because soon enough I'd be shuttling the children and their friends to a bewildering series of soccer games, soccer parties, soccer tournaments. I throw birthday parties with guest lists and budgets that approximate those of a wedding rehearsal dinner. The curious thing about this labor-intensive variety of parenting is that it has arisen now, when parents — and specifically mothers — have less time to devote to their children than ever before.

One can't help finding in these developments a frantic attempt to compensate for the hours some professional-class mothers spend away from their children. Mothering, which used to be a rather private affair (requiring, principally, a playpen, a backyard, a television set, and a coffeepot), has now adopted a very public dimension. Why, of course Sarah So-and-So is a good mother: little Andrew is at Gymboree, Music Rhapsody, Bright Child, and Fit for Kids every week! All of domestic life now turns on the entertainment and happiness not of the adults, but of the children.

Nowhere is this more evident than in the contemporary family vacation, as experienced by many members of the upper middle class. It is an intense experience, marked by numerous and often conflicting desires. Busy parents want to spend some uninterrupted time with their children, but they also desperately crave a substantial break from those children. Dad wants sex, but Mom has envisioned a precious interlude of near-monastic solitude.

Today's vacation would hardly qualify as one for the previous generation. As thrifty as my parents were, it would not have occurred to them to save money on a holiday by kipping in with their children. For them and many of their friends, the economics of travel were simple: if you couldn't afford two rooms at the good hotel, you took two rooms at the modest one, and if you couldn't afford two rooms there, you stayed home. The reasons for this were many, and the result was that even as a young child, I had a sense that my parents had a private life in which (how maddening!) I figured not at all, and in which they indulged in various puzzling adult pleasures, involving gin and tonic, and cigarettes, and perhaps — but how? — my mother's silky negligees. A tropical vacation was once so thoroughly associated with pleasures of the flesh and a kind of marital renewal incompatible with child care that little ones, on whom fine linens and outdoor dance floors would be wasted anyway, were often left home with a sitter.

But things are different now. Vacation days are few, and the frantic attempt to fuse sophisticated pleasure (a stay in an expensive hotel) with familial duty (making up for long nights at work with a one-week cram session, topic: the kids) means that whole families often occupy a single room at the toniest places. My husband and I don't drag our little boys through the Louvre, as I was dragged at a tender age (because my parents wanted to see it, and it would never have occurred to them to consult their children about where to go on holiday). Rather, we check into hotels with elaborate children's pools and nightly fireworks and huge duck ponds. It's all very jolly, but it is entirely possible, I suppose, that some parents will over-identify with the whole thing, will forget that they are in fact the adults and not the children. And if your conception of yourself is as a great big eight-year-old, you're not very likely to have sex on your mind come the end of the day.

When I was a teenager, in the seventies, I was always quite happy to accept a babysitting job, because I knew that once I got the kids to sleep, I could read *The Joy of Sex* for an hour or two. (I don't think I babysat for a single family that didn't have a copy.) There was a sense that young parents of that generation — granted, I grew up in Berkeley, which may have skewed the sample considerably — were still getting it on. Similarly the characters one encounters in Cheever and Updike, with their cocktails and cigarettes and affairs, seem at once infinitely more dissolute and more adult than most of the young parents I know. Nowadays American parents of a certain social class seem squeaky-clean, high-achieving, flush with cash, relatively exhausted, obsessed with their children, and somehow — how to pinpoint this? — undersexed.

If *I Don't Know How She Does It,* a book about a working woman who discovers deep joy and great sex by quitting her job and devoting herself to family life, had been written by a man, he would be the target of a lynch mob the proportions and fury of which would make Salman Rushdie feel like a lucky, lucky man. But of course it was written by a with-it female journalist, so it's safe, even admired. Allison Pearson, we have been given to understand, is telling it like it is. And what she's telling us, essentially, is that in several key aspects, the women's movement has been a bust, even for the social class that most ardently championed it.

Given the curious alchemy of feminism, which transforms absolutely anything women choose to do into a crucial element of liberation doctrine, confessing that one has given up sex has become a very right-on and empowering act. The notorious essay collection *The Bitch in the*

House is filled with such gleefully tendered admissions, including that of the writer Jill Bialosky, whose account of a long lunch with an old friend is featured on the book's jacket: "My friend asked me about my marriage. 'Are you guys having sex?' she asked bluntly. . . . I wanted to laugh." What's interesting about these public admissions is that they are utterly humiliating to husbands. Granted, Bialosky has protected her husband's privacy by referring to him as "D." throughout the essay. But perhaps, if her heart had really been in it, she would have written under a pseudonym.

Every account I've ever read in which a married woman admits that she's not having sex anymore begins with a red-hot account of the sex she used to have with her husband before they had children. Before Jill Bialosky decided to cut off poor D., he was having the time of his life. "He pressed up against me in dark alleys. I gave him blow jobs as he drove on one of our weekend treks. We made out in taxicabs. There was a kind of volatile tension wired through our relationship that set my body on fire feeling his arm resting against mine in the dark cavern of a movie theater."

But now? "A little faucet had turned off inside my body. My veins were cold. I didn't want to be touched." And here, with that little faucet, is the heart of the matter. The Jill Bialoskys of the world may feel that they belong to the most liberated group of women yet to stride the earth. These women assume that in the very act of confession, they are wearing the mantle of freedom. They are not only free enough to perform oral sex in a moving car — a bit of cutting-edge eroticism that, I believe, dates back to the Model T — but also free enough to admit, in tones of outrage and bewilderment, to the abrupt waning of their desire. What they don't understand, and what women of an earlier era might have been able to tell them, is that when the little faucet turns off, it is time not to rat out your husband (is there anything more wounding to a man, and therefore more cruel and vicious, than a wife's public admission that he is not satisfying her in bed?), but to *turn it back on*. It is not complicated; it requires putting the children to bed at a decent hour and adopting a good attitude. The rare and enviable woman is not the one liberated enough to tell hurtful secrets about her marriage to her girlfriends or the reading public. Nor is she the one capable of attracting the sexual attentions of a variety of worthy suitors. The rare woman — the good wife, and the happy one — is the woman who maintains her husband's sexual interest and who returns it in full measure.

Sex therapists concur that sexless marriages are not inherently problematic; if both partners are satisfied with a passionless union, the marriage is said to be in fine shape. But I'm not so sure. Marriage remains the most efficient engine of disenchantment yet invented. There is nothing like uninterrupted cohabitation and grinding responsibility to cast a clear, unforgiving light on the object of desire. Once children come along, it's easy for parents to regard each other as copresidents of an industrious little corporation. Certainly all sound marriages benefit from sudden and unexpected infusions of goodwill — *What luck! Here we are, so many years later, and still as happy as ever!* But the element that regularly restores a marriage to something with an aspect of romance rather than of collegiality is sex.

Housewife Confidential

THE SETTLEMENT" COOK BOOK begins, as cookbooks used to, with instructions on the proper way to run a household. To air a room: "Lower the upper sash of one window and raise the lower sash of an opposite window." To remove a glue stain: "Apply vinegar with a cloth." There are sections on the feeding of infants and of invalids: "Use the daintiest dishes in the house. Place a clean napkin on the tray and, if possible, a fresh flower."

My reaction to these household rules — and especially to the daily schedules for small children, which suggest thrilling mini-narratives of carefully lived days, of cooked cereal at seven o'clock and diluted orange juice at nine o'clock — is in the nature of avidity. The way a

45

lonely man in a motel room pores over *Playboy*, I pore over descriptions of ironing and kitchen routines. I have never made a solution composed of one part bleach and nine parts warm water, but the idea of such a solution and its many practical uses — wiping down an empty refrigerator once a month, sanitizing a kitchen sink — commands my riveted attention. The notion of a domestic life that purrs along, with schedules and order and carefully delineated standards, is endlessly appealing to me. It is also quite foreign, because I am not a housewife. I am an "at-home mother," and the difference between the two is vast.

Consider the etymology. When a woman described herself as a "housewife," she was defining herself primarily through her relationship to her house and her husband. That children came along with the deal was simply assumed, the way that airing rooms and occasionally cooking for invalids came along with the deal. When a housewife subjected herself and her work to a bit of brutally honest examination, she may have begun by assessing how well she was doing with the children, but she may just as well have begun by contemplating the nature and quality of her housework. If it had been suggested to her that she spend the long, delicate hours between three and six o'clock squiring her children to the array of enhancing activities pursued by the modern child, she would have laughed. Who would stay home to get dinner on?

More to the point, why had she chosen a house so close to a playground if the children weren't going to get out of her hair and play in it? The kind of childhood that many of us remember so fondly — with hours of free time and gangs of neighborhood kids meeting up after school — was possible partly because each block contained houses in which women were busy but close by, all too willing to push open a window and yell at the neighbor boy to get his fool bike out of the street.

But an at-home mother feels little obligation to the house itself. In fact she is keenly aware that the house can be a vehicle of oppression. She is "at home" only because that is where her children happen to be. She does not define herself through her housekeeping; if she is in any way solvent (and many at-home mothers are), she has, at the very least, a once-a-month cleaning woman to do the most onerous tasks. (That some of the most significant achievements of the women's movement — specifically, liberation from housework and child care — have been bought at the expense of poor women, often of poor brown-skinned women, is a bitter irony that very few feminists will discuss directly, other than to murmur something vague about "universal day care" and then, on reflex, blame the Republicans.)

The at-home mother defines herself by her relationship to her children. She is making sacrifices on their behalf, giving up a career to give them something only she can. Her No. 1 complaint concerns the issue of respect: She demands it! Can't get enough of it! She isn't like a fifties housewife: ironing curtains, shampooing the carpets, stuck. She knows all about those women. She has seen *Pleasantville* and watched *Leave It to Beaver;* she's made more June Cleaver jokes than she can count. (In fact June Cleaver — a character on a television show that went off the air in 1963 — looms over her to a surprising extent, a sickening, terrifying specter: *Is that how people think I spend my time?*) If she has seen Todd Haynes's sumptuously beautiful movie *Far From Heaven,* she understands and agrees wholeheartedly with the film's implication: that being a moneyed white housewife, with full-time help, in pre–Betty Friedan Hartford, Connecticut, was just as oppressive and soul-withering as being a black man in pre–civil rights Hartford. The at-home mother's attitude toward housewives of the fifties and sixties is a mixture of pity, outrage on their behalf, and gently mocking humor. (I recently received a birthday card that featured a perfectly coiffed fifties housewife standing in a gleaming kitchen. "The smart woman knows her way around the kitchen," the front of the card said. Inside: "Around the kitchen, out the back door, and to a decent restaurant.")

The at-home mother has a lot on her mind; to a significant extent, she has herself on her mind. She must not allow herself to shrivel up with boredom. She must do things *for herself*. She must get to the gym, the spa, the yoga studio. To the book group. (She wouldn't be caught dead setting up tables and filling nut cups for a bridge party — June Cleaver! June Cleaver! — but a book group, which blends an agreeable seriousness of purpose with the kind of busy chitchat that women the world over adore, is irresistible.) She must go to lunch with like-minded friends, and to the movies. She needs to feed herself intellectually and emotionally; she needs to be on guard against exhaustion. She must find a way to combine the traditional women's work of child rearing with the kind of shared housework arrangements and domestic liberation that working mothers enjoy. Most important, she must somehow draw a line in the sand between the valuable, important work she is doing and the pathetic imprisonment, the *Doll's House* existence, of the housewife of old. It's a tall order.

Several years ago, the Hollywood producer Lynda Obst wrote a *Los Angeles Times* column in which she decried the tendency of upper-level female studio executives to quit their jobs once they became mothers. "Doesn't anyone remember how painfully poignant it was to grow up with a brilliant mother stuck in the suburbs with nothing to do?" she implored. This, of course, is the politically correct attitude about such women. The general idea, implied in countless books and articles and in a variety of popular movies, is that shortly after President Truman dropped the big one on Nagasaki, an entire generation of brave, brilliant women — many of them enjoying the deep satisfaction of doing shift work in munitions factories (the extent to which the riveters' lot is glorified by professional-class feminists who have never set foot on a factory floor is shameful) — was kidnapped by a bunch of rat-bastard men, deposited in Levittown, and told to mop. That women in large numbers were eagerly, joyfully complicit in this life plan, that women helped to create the plan, is rarely considered.

To be a young woman during the war years was to know that many of the boys from your high school class were overseas and, perhaps, that several of them had died there. It was to have a steady, often unspoken fear that a future including children and a husband and a household — women used to be unconflicted and unashamed about wanting these things — might not be in the cards. For it all to change on a dime — for the men to come home in vast, apparently unscathed numbers, and for there to be the GI Bill and GI mortgages and plenty of good jobs for returning servicemen (remember, these were women who had experienced childhoods in which there were not enough jobs, in which it was highly possible for a family to be ruined) — must have been a relief beyond measure. That women, en masse, reconsidered their plan in fairly short order — *The Feminine Mystique* was published within twenty years of V-J Day — also gets scant mention. The postwar housewife era, whether one views it with horror or nostalgia, was short-lived.

Hollywood has a curious double obsession these days: lionizing the World War II serviceman and demonizing the fifties husband. What the brain trust fails to grasp is that he is the same man. The central heartbreaker of *Saving Private Ryan* is that Tom Hanks never makes it home to his adored wife. But if he'd gotten back to Pennsylvania in one piece, he would have been just another pot roast–demanding, afternoon-newspaper-reading monster like Ward Cleaver (who was an engineer with the Seabees before dragging poor June off to his lair). Husbands lurk menacingly in the backgrounds of so many contemporary works set during the housewife period, emanating a threatening maleness (just the ticket at Normandy, but oh well), tramping their dirty feet across freshly scrubbed linoleum, demanding sex and clean laundry and subservience. In Michael Cunningham's spare and excellent novel *The Hours,* Laura Brown, a postwar California housewife so stultified by her lot that she ends up going cuckoo, kissing a neighbor lady, and eventually abandoning her children, must endure a day in which the responsibilities to her war hero husband include not only the hellish complexity of baking a cake from scratch but also marital relations, an activity that forces her to make the ultimate sacrifice: putting a bookmark in *Mrs. Dalloway.* "There will be no reading tonight," the narrator informs us ominously.

(Was Laura too oppressed to switch on the bedside lamp after the brute had been satisfied? Apparently so.)

Most curious about all of these representations is that they run so completely counter to my experience of housewives. I was raised by a housewife; my friends' mothers were housewives. Many of them, in retrospect, seemed mildly depressed. Perhaps full-time employment would have alleviated that depression quickly and completely (although the number of working mothers I know who are at sheer wits' end makes me question that central assumption of the women's movement). But what I remember most clearly about those housewives is not their ennui, but their competence. They never served takeout for dinner; they cooked dinner — a protein, a starch, two vegetables, and dessert. They knew how to iron and mend, and how to cope with the endless series of domestic crises that unseat me on a daily basis: the unraveled sweater sleeve, the chocolate stain on the tiny button-down shirt, the expensive set of sheets with the torn hem, the child who turns up with a raging fever two minutes before the Christmas pageant, the husband who announces that he'd like to invite someone from work to dinner that night.

I would like to be the kind of woman who can cope — easily, effortlessly, while gabbing away about something else altogether — with all those things. I'm not. I'm an at-home mother, far too educated and uppity to have knuckled down and learned anything about stain removal or knitting or stretching recipes. My mother tried to teach me, and God knows I was a rapt student (like most adult obsessions, mine has its roots in childhood experience), but my attention kept attaching itself to the least important part of the lesson. "Now I'm ironing the placket," she would say, and I would stand beside her, thinking, *Placket. Good word*. Perhaps I didn't have a great enough sense of urgency. I knew there were college and perhaps graduate school to contend with before I'd need to know how to line a baking sheet with rice paper. And as it turned out, by the time I had a household of my own, the world had changed. I have been married a total of sixteen years to a total of two men, and never once have I been asked to iron a single item of either man's clothing or to replace even one popped button, for which I suppose I have the women's movement to thank. But I realize now, late in the game, that we'd be much better off if I had a few of those skills.

Housewives, however, were not concerned solely with housework. Once I asked my mother why she didn't go to PTA meetings. She said, "That's for women who don't have anything better to do with their time." She was a housewife through and through, yet she had a sense of herself — highly accurate — as a purposefully busy woman. One reason that the women's movement took off in this country the way it did was that its organizers eventually realized that housewives were capable not only of weeping into their teacups and trying to name their unnameable problem but also of political action. In fact, they had a long history of political action.

Consider the League of Women Voters, which during the period in question was mostly made up of non-employed, college-educated mothers married to professional men. These were women who cooked the family breakfast and sent the children off to school with packed lunch boxes, and then vacuumed their lovely living rooms and used them to host not book groups, but, rather, meetings on civil rights initiatives and opposition to the Vietnam War. These meetings tended to be somewhat proper and highly ladylike. They were run by women who had learned the finer points of parliamentary procedure in their college sororities. They were attended by women who had a firm belief in the civilizing power of combed hair and fresh lipstick and not talking out of turn. These were women, one might argue, badly in need of a consciousness-raising session. But if a truly raised consciousness includes an awareness of the injustice done to others and a willingness to try to stop it, then these women were at least halfway there.

Housewives were the people who put Trick-or-Treat for UNICEF boxes in millions of small hands. They were, of course, thrifty (thrift is the signal virtue of the housewife), but many of them were also high-minded, convinced that people ought to help one another out. George Harrison may have held a concert for Bangladesh, but it was the mothers on my block who sat down and wrote little checks — ten dollars, fifteen dollars — to CARE. Many housewives shared a belief in the power of boycotts, which could so easily be conducted while grocery shopping. I remember hearing my mother's half of a long, complicated telephone conversation about whether it would or would not undermine the housewives' beef strike of 1973 if the caller defrosted and cooked meat bought prior to the strike.

Tucked into the aforementioned copy of *"The Settlement" Cook Book,* along with handwritten recipes for Chocolate Diamonds and Oma's German Cheesecake, is a small card that reads FREEDOM AND JUSTICE FOR J.P. STEVENS WORKERS. The organizers of that long-ago boycott understood two things: first, that if you were going to cripple a supplier of household goods (J.P. Stevens manufactured table linens, hosiery, and blankets), you had to enlist housewives; and second, that you stood a better chance of catching their attention if you printed your slogan on the reverse of a card that contained a table of common metric equivalents — a handy, useful reminder that 1 liter = 1 quart and also that the makers of Finesse hosiery exploited their workers.

The success of the women's movement depended on imposing a certain narrative — of boredom, of oppression, of despairing uselessness — on an entire generation of women. This narrative has only gained strength as the years have passed, leaving people with a skewed and rather offensive view of those women. Consider the case of the most famous housewife of the era: Erma Bombeck. To think about her life in any depth is to realize that even the most "typical" housewife of them all — *Erma Bombeck* — led a life of infinitely greater complexity, worth, and dignity than any of the modern mythologizers, with their subdued and shrinking heroines, could imagine.

Like many housewives of her day, Bombeck had a rough Depression childhood, in Dayton, Ohio. Her father was a crane operator who died suddenly when she was nine. Her mother — who had left school after sixth grade, married at fourteen, and given birth to her only child at sixteen — lost their house and their furniture. Together they moved into a front bedroom in her grandparents' house, and Erma Senior got a factory job. "One day you were a family," Bombeck recalled, "living in a little house at the bottom of a hill. The next day it was all gone." Erma Senior, a frustrated stage mother, sent her daughter to tap-dancing lessons and pushed her into contests and radio appearances. (The tap-dancing craze of the thirties was so powerful that a few minutes of frantic dancing by a girl Shirley Temple's age was the stuff even of a successful radio spot.)

Young Erma's inclinations ran in a different direction.

She was clever and bookish; she loved James Thurber and Robert Benchley and H. Allen Smith. When Erma was fourteen, the famous newspaper correspondent Dorothy Thompson came to Dayton, and Erma — even though she was coming down with the measles — persuaded her mother to let her attend Thompson's lecture. ("I infected the entire hall that night," she remembered.) For Christmas she asked for and received an expensive book by Thompson. Not surprisingly, given the times and her station in life, she attended a vocational high school, which required students to spend two weeks a month pursuing a "commercial alternate." She must not have been particularly interested in the kind of department store and telephone company jobs usually recommended for girls, because in a burst of chutzpah and innocence, she wangled an interview with the managing editor of the *Dayton Journal-Herald*. She impressed him (one doesn't like to trade in clichés, but it's impossible to imagine the scene without the word *spunk* coming into play), but he said he had only one job opening, and it was a full-time position. On the spot she talked him into hiring a friend for the other two weeks a month, and so, at age fifteen and with the title "copy girl" (hardly sexist, considering its opposite), she began her newspaper career.

Let us pause for a moment to consider how the story already diverges from the standard cant. Apparently it was possible, long before Rosie tied on her kerchief and flexed her fetching biceps, for a woman to get factory work when she needed to support her family. It was also possible for a young girl to nurture dreams of a professional career, and for her to find — decades before Take Our Daughters to Work Day — a female role model already pursuing that work. It was possible for a bright, quick-thinking girl to storm as emphatically male an environment as a city newspaper and to create the exact kind of job-sharing arrangement that contemporary working mothers think they invented. Most important, it was possible in those days for a girl to overcome a considerable amount of adversity — poverty, and the early loss of a father, and a tight net of employment law clearly intended to favor men — to make something of herself.

It was also possible to do all these things and still dream of children and of staying home to raise them. Erma had met a young reporter, Bill Bombeck, and after he returned from the service, in 1948, they married. Erma by then had a college degree and had been promoted at the *Journal-Herald,* from part-time to full-time copy girl and then to full-fledged newspaperwoman. She became friends with the reporter Phyllis Battelle, who remembered "a bouncy kid in bobbysocks, knife-pleated skirts and baggy sweaters." But what Erma really wanted was children: "Putting on panty hose every morning is just not whoopee time. My dream was to putter around the house, learn how to snap beans, put up curtains and bake bread." Finally, through the adoption of the Bombecks' first child, their purchase of a house in a subdivision outside Dayton, and Erma's resignation from the newspaper, those dreams came true. And she began to go absolutely bonkers.

In her best book, the memoir *A Marriage Made in Heaven . . . Or Too Tired for an Affair* (1993), she reports that the women of the suburbs were all "bored out of their skulls." In driveways and supermarket parking lots, "[we] commiserated among ourselves as to what we had gotten ourselves into." What she needed, she soon realized — without benefit of *Working Mother* magazine or even a single book about achieving "work/life balance" — was a job. And with no fuss or fanfare (much the way my own mother did, when she realized she couldn't spend another afternoon washing the kitchen walls and climbed off the stepladder to take a curious look at the "Help Wanted: Female" section of the *San Francisco Chronicle*), she got one: editing the local shopping circular. In 1964, not long after her youngest child boarded the school bus bound for kindergarten, she combed her hair, braced herself, and asked the editor of her community's weekly newspaper for a job as a housewife columnist. Success came quickly, and it never left. She was soon back at the *Journal-Herald,* where, within three weeks of her return, her columns were syndicated nationally. A sensation.

The idea of a "housewife" — at least of the American

postwar variety — was forged by writers like Bombeck, who codified the essential characteristics of the type: good-natured, comically rueful about the physical indignities of aging, harassed into the end of time yet capable of moments of transcendence, when she was struck by the power of her love for her children and by the importance of her sacrifice on their behalf.

Unlike the contemporary at-home mother, who tends to demonize her counterparts, Bombeck championed working mothers. She never questioned either their motivations for working or their love for their children. Indeed her writing is refreshingly apolitical on the subject. Still, she was keenly aware of the two difficulties mothers have always faced when they have chosen to work: that their maternal inclinations will be considered suspect, and that the resulting decline in domestic standards will be much more of a burden to themselves than to their husbands.

"I discovered something else about guilt," she wrote about going back to work in the sixties.

There were exceptions. If you spent time away from your family delivering thirty empty egg cartons for the Christmas bazaar project or volunteering for playground duty, you were exempt from guilt. However, if you held down a part-time job somewhere that took you out of the house for a few hours, you were pursuing your selfish interests and were a bad mother. The operative word here seemed to be "money." If you got paid for something, it was bad for the children.

Was Bombeck's husband furious that she had decided to jump ship, shaming him as a man incapable of supporting his own family? Not at all, she said; he "was proud of my career." Her sorrows were self-inflicted and immediately recognizable to today's working mother:

> The guilt I felt was self-inflicted. As long as I was fussy about my kids' peanut butter, I could say yes to the commencement speech on Mother's Day. If I made a tuna noodle casserole and left a note to my daughter to slide it in a 350-degree oven and brought her a present when I came home in time for dinner, I could do the Mike Douglas show. As long as my husband smelled his bath towel and looked like he had just seen God, I felt I was allowed to pursue a career for another week. To complain would have left me open for, "No one asked you to work. You can quit any time."

Jean Kerr experienced many of the same sentiments. She had achieved extraordinary success with *Please Don't Eat the Daisies* (1957) almost a decade before Bombeck began writing her column. The book located a kind of boredom and silent desperation, leavened by mirth and the sweetness of motherhood, that resonated with the experiences of millions of women. Kerr wrote about motherhood with the kind of cheerful cynicism that once marked the condition: "The thing about having a baby — and I can't be the first person to have noticed this — is that thereafter you *have* it, and it's years before you can distract it from any elemental needs by saying, 'Oh for Heaven's sake, go look at the television.'"

Like Bombeck, Kerr occupies a spot in the modern imagination as yet another example of a repressed housewife whose lot could have been transformed if she'd had a job to give her an identity, to wrest her from her husband's stalag, where she served as the combination of cook and comfort girl. Once again the myth is dead wrong. In the book's introduction, Kerr observes that she had located her life's true goal at the age of three. To be a wife and mother? No, to sleep in until noon. Toward that end she had become a playwright, which she continued doing after her children were born, and diverted her income toward her worthy cause: "I was now paying the salary of a very nice girl who pretended to enjoy distributing pablum and crayons until I emerged, rosy and wrinkled, at eleven in the morning."

Shirley Jackson trod similar ground in *Raising Demons* (1957), a book whose jacket cover — happy children surrounding a pull-toy duck — is as far from the spirit of

"The Lottery" as it is possible to get. Jackson was also the author of *Special Delivery* (1960), the title page of which describes it as "a useful book for brand-new mothers in which Shirley Jackson as chief resident provides a sane and sage approach to the hilarious and homey situations which accompany the advent of motherhood." In those days a woman understood that she would have to shape her life's professional and intellectual ambitions around the unwavering demands of motherhood. The housewife writers regarded their work in much the same way that middle-class husbands of the era regarded theirs: tedious, rarely glamorous, and necessary to the support and nurture of their families — institutions that they regarded, although they would never have said as much, as their lives' great achievements.

Any serious study of housewife writers must include Peg Bracken, who wrote her best-known books during the early sixties, when the women's movement was still a sleeping giantess. Her attitude toward the housewife's lot, however, is not unconflicted: the titles of her two most famous books are *The I Hate to Cook Book* (1960) and *The I Hate to Housekeep Book* (1962). Her writing reveals her to be a cheerful sort, possessed of a winsome prose style. She is, she confesses, "but destiny's plaything," and her approach to housewifery combines whimsy and practicality. (The accompanying Hilary Knight illustrations capture the spirit of the text with a precision not seen since the great days of the nineteenth-century illustrated novel.) Her jolliness may well have had something to do with the fact that she clearly liked her hooch. *The I Hate to Cook Book* was written, she tells us, "for those of us who want to fold our big dishwater hands around a dry Martini instead of a wet flounder, come the end of a long day." Powdered milk, she once observed, is preferable to the real McCoy not only because it is cheaper but also because it can be a component of "a good frothy punch," one consisting of "milk, egg, sugar, whisky, beaten with an electric mixer."

Bracken's feelings about her domestic work take the form of good-hearted acquiescence, although some of her books' most offhand humor reveals the edge of genuine despair. The recipe for Skid Row Stroganoff, for instance, includes the instruction, "Add the flour, salt, paprika, and mushrooms, stir, and let it cook five minutes while you light a cigarette and stare sullenly at the sink." (One hesitates to wander into the minefield of literary biography, but I find it impossible to read *The I Hate to Cook Book* without dwelling on the fact that while Bracken was writing it, her husband told her it was the stupidest idea for a book he'd ever heard of. They divorced four years later.)

Although Bracken's collected works are slightly less explicitly political than those of Beatrix Potter, anyone taking the historical long view can easily discover within them the seeds of the revolution that would soon be upon this country. How else to account for the fact that a book on housekeeping contains a chapter on coping with depression? "Every girl owes it to herself to hang onto her mind as long as she can," we learn in that chapter, which is called "How to Be Happy When You're Miserable." "If the fulfillment of your own purposes seems to be flickering," she writes, one ought to remember that many high achievers — Daumier, say, or Ogilby, who translated Homer and Virgil — got a late start. Women frustrated by the demands of motherhood ought to remember that "there is world enough and time," a bit of counsel as useful to the full-time mothers of today as to those of forty years ago. In fact, I found several bits of sound advice in *The I Hate to Housekeep Book,* among them, "Each time you give the house a good going-over, start with a different room" and "Act immediately on whatever housewifely impulses come your way." (And, if I might add my own two cents on matters domestic, if you substitute the word *sexual* for the word *housewifely,* you also end up with the best approach to conjugal relations I have hit upon thus far.)

What is refreshing about the housewife writers is their candor about the tedium of raising children. Although the at-home mother must think of the work as exalted (otherwise why isn't she back at the law firm, bringing home the big bucks?), housewives were willing to admit that the enterprise was often an emotional bust. And no one was more willing than Erma Bombeck, who, to be at once current and crass, "branded" the form. Why she was the one to have such out-of-the-park success with the subject has less to do with her prose than with the sheer force of her personality, her eye for the precise and homey detail, and her matchless way with a gag. I had expected to reread her work with a gentle, reminiscing smile and was amazed by how often I found myself laughing. I do not want, however, to misrepresent her writing. She was, to a certain extent, a hack. How could she not have been? To write that frequently (she had written well in excess of four thousand columns by the time of her death in 1996), on such tight deadlines and with such a tightly circum-scribed length, is almost by definition to rely on formulas, to repeat oneself, to tread a few good one-liners almost to death.

Even a true-blue fan will be shocked by Bombeck's almost shameless willingness to trot out the same jokes and observations over and over again. Certainly her work achieved maximal effect in its original context: meted out regularly but sparingly, in seven-hundred-word doses on the women's page — snappy, chin-up reminders that every-one hates doing the laundry and that even the most adored children can run you ragged with frustration and boredom.

In those days, no matter where you lived or what your local newspaper was, the women's page was firmly in the hands of a group of stalwart midwesterners. I grew up in Berkeley, where the front page often informed me of unsettling events close to home, of riots on Telegraph Avenue and of the Black Panthers (Huey Newton was once an honored guest speaker at a public school I attended) and later of the Symbionese Liberation Army. But the back of the newspaper — a respite — gave me Erma and also the Iowans Abby and Ann, and the Minnesotan Charles Schulz. (Bil Keane, the creator of *The Family Circus*, was from the East, but he and Erma became neighbors and great pals.) They all seemed connected to the fabric of an America that I didn't live in but believed in passionately, a place in which "student unrest" was rarely mentioned, in which the central elements of the national consciousness weren't up for complete reassessment and rejection, in which most of life's difficulties could be handled with a combination of good humor and endurance, and in which graver matters were quickly dispatched by scheduling an appointment with one's "pastor or clergyman."

Read collectively, Bombeck's pieces offer a startlingly precise chronicle of her time. Anyone in search of a good topic for a women's studies dissertation would do well to take a look at Bombeck's columns. It would be difficult to find a more comprehensive overview of the way middle-class women lived their lives — and of the way their lives changed — during the seventies and eighties. "Lady, you *are* the problem," a member of the women's liberation movement once wrote to her. In fact she was not. She was a talented woman who had once dreamed of working for the *New York Times* and who ended up as one of the best-known figures in American journalism. She was a woman who combined work and motherhood as gracefully as it is possible to do so, who championed working and at-home mothers with equal ardor, and who campaigned tirelessly for the Equal Rights Amendment. (Her close friend Liz Carpenter, a press secretary for Lady Bird Johnson, recalls that the two were "the Thelma and Louise of the ERA.")

There is no one my mother would less want to be compared to than Erma Bombeck, whose work — as far as I know — she never read. My mother was an accomplished hostess, a flirt, a reader. Her sensibilities were in no way midwestern. Yet in the four years since her death, I have rarely remembered her more vividly than when I read all that Bombeck a few months back. In part this has to do with the simple household economies of the time, which I had forgotten about but of which Bombeck was a faithful recorder. To read Bombeck is to find a constantly updated economic index of her day: the problem with a bathtub faucet left on the "shower" position is that it ruins an eight-dollar hairdo; the problem with a bored child's deciding to put lime wedges in glasses of soda pop is that limes cost $1.49 a pound. I don't think I ever spent a day with my mother — even late in her life, when her fortunes had improved considerably — when she didn't mention the price of something. Like Bombeck and a lot of other housewives of her generation, she grew up poor in hard times, which she never discussed but never forgot. Like Bombeck, she kept the household accounts, and she was careful about them. I grew up in the most solidly middle-class academic family you can imagine, but every couple of months my mother would borrow a bottle-capping contraption so that she could put up her own root beer — made from Hires elixir, absolutely delicious, and roundly complimented by my father for its pennies-a-glass economy. As for me, child of my time, I could not tell you the price of a single item in my refrigerator. All I know — from long, unpleasant precedent — is that much of it is going bad and headed for the trash can.

But what reminds me most of my mother is harder to pinpoint. It has to do with the way both women dealt with motherhood, which is for me an exquisitely over-wrought enterprise, full of guilt-racked, sleepless nights and over-worried-about children and the never-ending sense that I'm doing too little or too much or the wrong thing, or missing the crucial moments, or somehow warping these perfect creatures that my body — that witless dud — had sense enough to knit together but my heart and mind can't seem to figure out how to raise with my mother's unworried ease. Housewives didn't trot after their children the way I trot after mine: Junior All-Stars! Karate! Art for Tots! Their children trotted after them. I whiled away a childhood leaning on the counters of dry cleaners and shoe repairmen, and I was happy to do it. I liked being with my mother. To me, she never seemed diminished or unimportant because of those endless domestic errands. On the contrary, the work she did was wholly connected to the life we were living. The notes my father took on the flyleaf of *Howards End* apparently got translated into words spoken in a lecture hall I could hardly imagine; but the steak my mother spent five minutes choosing showed up on my plate that night.

If you asked any of the mothers of my acquaintance how motherhood has changed us, we would tell you — in one way or another — that it has introduced into our lives an almost unbearably powerful form of love and also a ceaseless, grinding anxiety, one that often propels us to absurd activities. (I know a working mother who FedExed breast milk home from a business trip. I recently hosted a birthday party for thirty-two children because I couldn't arrive at any sensible way to compose a guest list.) For many of us this transformation has included a helpless sense of repeated failures, both large and small.

For the women of an earlier generation, however, motherhood brought a clear and compelling awareness of human vulnerability, and a sense of having somehow been charged with the care of others. I can remember my mother faithfully cutting the wrappers off cans of dog food because if she sent in enough of them, the manufacturer would make a contribution to Guide Dogs for the Blind. I myself have compassion fatigue and have limited my "charitable giving" to a certain few circumscribed causes. At the back of Erma Bombeck's last book, published after her death from complications following a kidney transplant, is an organ donor card that the reader can fill out, along with information on the Erma Bombeck Organ Donor Awareness Project. I keep meaning to fill that card out; my mother would have done it in an instant, without thinking twice about it. But I'm a busy woman — my children are two-sport athletes at age seven — and I haven't gotten around to it yet.

A Necessary Person

For the long nights you lay awake
And watched for my unworthy sake:
For your most comfortable hand
That led me through uneven land:
For all the storybooks you read:
For all the pains you comforted:
For all you pitied, all you bore,
In sad and happy times of yore:
My second mother, my first wife,
The angel of my infant life —
From the sick child, now well and old,
Take, nurse, the little book you hold!

— ROBERT LOUIS STEVENSON

I DIDN'T KNOW a single child who had a nanny when I was growing up. I knew babysitters, of course, and I someday hoped to be one myself. In eighth grade I stayed after school for six consecutive Thursday afternoons so that I could take the Red Cross babysitting class, slipping a weighted doll in and out of a plastic tub of warm water, patting its back in anticipation of an imaginary burp, testing warmed milk on my wrist. But nannies were not babysitting teenagers. They were exotics, a special breed from long-ago times, characters in English nursery rhymes or in the faraway worlds of royalty and the rich. Although I had no personal experience of nannies, I knew what a nanny would wear, how she would behave, what her duties would be, how she would learn about available positions, and how she would conduct herself during a job interview. I knew these things because I had seen *Mary Poppins.*

Released in 1964, and rereleased in 1973 and 1980, the impact of *Mary Poppins* on my generation is hard to overstate. We grew up in an America in which nannies were as unfamiliar to middle-class neighborhoods as Jaguars and Martians. But we would become adults in an America that had invented a new nanny culture. To an astonishing extent, the way we came to think and talk about our employees was shaped by the movie we had seen so many years earlier. Nannies have become a force in American life because of the three-decade-long influx of middle-class mothers to the work force, and the more recent wave of cheap female immigrant labor. "She's the Guatemalan Mary Poppins!" a working mother will happily announce of her new employee — or the Colombian or the Caribbean one. It's hard to find a book or an article about hiring a nanny that doesn't make mention of the old girl. And even though the culture and experience of a third world child care provider are as removed from those of an Edwardian nanny as it is possible to be, we understand what the reference means: the nanny is good, she's kind, and her ability to transform a chaotic household into a place of order and contentment verges on the supernatural. What we are also implicitly saying, however unwittingly, is that she doesn't threaten us. She won't steal our children's love from us.

• • •

AND SO IT COMES as a shock when a person my age (a person who has herself employed Honduras's answer to Mary Poppins) introduces the movie to her own children and discovers that it's hardly an endorsement for hiring a nanny.

What people remember about the movie is that the family finds happiness and the nanny is magical. What they misremember is that it's a film with a surprising moral: fire the nanny. In a sense, *Mary Poppins* is an anti-nanny propaganda film, the *Reefer Madness* of the working-mother set.

•   •   •

IN A CERTAIN SENSE, calling today's immigrant nanny a "Mary Poppins" is entirely appropriate. Both the proper British nanny and the contemporary third world child care provider entered their lines of work because of the confluence of an identical set of social forces: a sudden rise in the population of poor women; a concomitant rise in the number of rich ones; and a radical reshaping of middle-class family life, which necessitated the use of servants who specialized in the care and upbringing of children. In every culture in the world, wherever rich and poor coexist, it will not take long for them to figure out what to do with each other. In such circumstances, a servant class will always evolve.

In our time and place, the forces that bring nanny and employer together are, respectively, the collapse of the third world, which has flooded the United States with immigrants desperate for work; the rise of the two-career couple, which has doubled the income of many professional-class families and created the large-scale need for child care; and an intense preoccupation with the emotional lives of children, which puts a premium on top-quality care for them.

Similarly, in Victorian England, a booming mercantile economy washed cash through the English non-nobility at a terrific rate, creating the largest and most powerful middle class the world had yet seen. At the same time, the population swelled because of improvements in women's health and a decline in infant mortality. Millions of the agrarian poor, desperate for work, traveled to the big cities, where large middle-class households were in need of servants. The Victorian cults of childhood and motherhood, not so unlike our own, transformed the nursery into a place of great importance, over which the nanny ruled supreme.

●　　　●　　　●

ALTHOUGH WE TEND to think of the British nanny — formally trained, bred to the job, imperious, unflappable, and immaculately turned out — as one of England's oldest traditions, she was actually a relatively short-lived institution. Born in the early days of Victoria's reign, when industrialization and a population explosion among both the poor and the middle class brought the two groups together in a highly regimented and hierarchical servant culture, she had all but disappeared by the end of the Second World War. The middle-class house that was populated with specialized servants became a thing of the past, and nannies evolved into an accoutrement strictly of upper-class life, associated with the aristocracy.

In the early seventies the English historian Jonathan Gathorne-Hardy realized that if any formal study of the nanny was to include extensive interviews with the women themselves, as well as with their former charges, it would need to be done at once: the nannies were by then in their dotage. And so he began an investigation that resulted in *The Rise and Fall of the British Nanny,* a mesmerizing work of social history that captures the world of nanny, mistress, and charges in precise and captivating prose.

The book describes a world as different from our own as it is possible to be — a world of butlers and footmen and ladies' maids, and the astonishing formality that governed their codes of dress and comportment:

> To prevent anarchy among the armies of their domestic servants, the Victorians imposed a rigid system of rules, hierarchies, uniforms, functions, promotions, and so on; a code of discipline which was almost military both in strictness and in its multifarious subdivision. It was in this context that the institution of the nanny grew firm. Between 1850 and 1880 her place in the household, her power, her duties, her clothing, her training, were all well-defined.

Servants are the world's great snobs, and nannies were ferocious ones. By the beginning of the Edwardian period, the nanny rivaled only the valet and the head housekeeper in status. These were the only three servants who reported directly to their employer and not to someone else in service. The nanny's stature grew when nanny training colleges began to open around England. The most highly respected of these was the formidable Norland School, whose program was intended to "offer a new career to gentlewomen by birth and education, and to girls of good education and refinement." This was, of course, overstatement — nannies were working-class — but it was an appealing notion to both the girls and their future employers. When Norland graduates headed off for their first positions, the school's founder, Mrs. Ward, tellingly advised them, "Nurses — take your silver-backed hairbrushes to impress the servants."

•   •   •

THE ENGLISH NURSERY was separated by a "muffling green baize door" from the rest of the household, in an attic room. Nannies and their charges lived neither among the servants nor among the householders, emphasizing the notion that childhood was now considered a distinct and separate sphere. Children were presented to their mothers and fathers once a day, in the evening, the audience preceded by a "frenzy of brushing and washing and dressing." In this system of raising children, the mother tended to become a somewhat glamorous and mysterious figure — an allure conferred on her by the distance maintained in the household. As a result children often adored their mothers in the distant, romantic way that people adore movie stars.

Such love was easily returned. As Gathorne-Hardy aptly observes of the English mother during this period, "After all it was not so difficult for them. They had none of the wear and tear of bringing up children, or indeed of anything else." I sometimes wonder if my love for my children — so powerful as to be indescribable — is not in some measure a product of similar forces. It's easy to fall helplessly, sentimentally, almost romantically in love with one's children when they aren't harassing you every moment, binding you to the kitchen and laundry room, and drowning all of your worldly promise in their incessant, labor-intensive demands.

Gathorne-Hardy's description of the relationships between nannies and "their" children — at once enchanting and heartbreaking — ranks among the most powerful accounts of family life that I've ever read. He speaks of grown men who remained stoically dry-eyed when discussing the deaths of their mothers, but who dissolved into tears when discussing their nannies. On visits home such men frequently dashed past the drawing room where their parents sat waiting and tore up three flights of stairs to visit Nanny in her nursery. It was common for public school boys, sent off at the age of seven, to cry not for their mothers, but for their nannies, who tended to mourn their charges' departure as they would a death.

•   •   •

AFTER WORLD WAR II this way of life came to an end. English middle-class mothers raised their own children, while across the ocean American war brides began producing armies of children. As both sets of mothers found themselves up to their elbows in soiled play clothes and mashed bananas, they yearned, as only a mother of small children can, for a bit of peace and a measure of freedom. It was in this new context that the idea of a nanny became the object of curiosity and fantasy.

The first people to realize that there might be a potential market for stories involving nannies and their charges were Bruce and Beatrice Gould, the husband and wife publishers of *Ladies' Home Journal*. They had in mind a series of articles about Princesses Margaret and Elizabeth, young women with whom Americans had become enraptured. (It is hard to believe anymore, but when Elizabeth was young she was strikingly pretty, with a wide, lipsticked smile and a tiny waist. Margaret was beautiful and a clotheshorse, a proto-Diana.) In looking for the right person to write the series, the Goulds came across the perfect narrator: Marion Crawford, who had been the girls' governess for seventeen years, and who had recently retired, married, and moved into a grace-and-favor cottage on the grounds of Kensington Palace.

Crawford adored the royal family in the kind of near-hysterical way that senior-level servants often do. Their smallest tokens of affection and esteem meant everything to her, so the question of why she decided to betray them so spectacularly — her book is fawning, but it is also the first of the intimate exposés that have long since become the bane of the royal family — remains one of publishing's great mysteries.

In 1951 *The Little Princesses* appeared in installments in the magazine and later was published as a book. It became an immediate sensation, an international bestseller that would be reprinted and rediscovered every few years — and for good reason: it's terrific. Novelistic and carefully plotted, it has the pitch-perfect attention to the kinds of details — of dress and food and the specifics of housekeeping on the grandest level imaginable — that have appealed to female readers for more than half a century. Moreover, it is set within the context of a series of riveting historic events that would change the fate of the monarchy, and particularly of Elizabeth, who as a serious, kindhearted child never imagined that she would one day be queen of England.

The Little Princesses centers on that great subject, the progress of a girl. It is Elizabeth's story, and we see her moving unknowingly, but inexorably, toward her future. Crawford began her tenure when Elizabeth's father was merely the Duke of York, a good-hearted, childlike fellow who liked nothing more than a game of rousing hopscotch or a cozy night by the fire working on his needlepoint. (When he grew frustrated filling in the background, Crawfie would take over, allowing him to work on the more interesting parts of the image.) He had no expectation of ever becoming the sovereign and had settled into a cozy life with a wife who adored him and two little girls who were themselves demon hopscotchers. The narrative is thus propelled by a series of exciting and dramatic events: Edward VIII's abdication in 1936, George VI's sudden coronation, the family's move to Buckingham Palace — and then, the war.

The family's astonishing bravery during the bombing of London transformed them in the public eye, catapulting them from members of a dynasty of waning importance into embodiments of the ancient role of kings: to ally the country's greatest power with its weakest citizens. Like all great histories, *The Little Princesses* ends with a wedding, Elizabeth's to Philip Mountbatten, and finally with a peek ahead to her role as mother: Charles, her first child, was born just before Crawfie left the family's employ.

The book has never been considered more than a popular sensation, but the writing is wonderful — clear and unsentimental — and its descriptions of nursery life are often profound. "It is impossible," Crawford says, "to convey to anyone who has not known it the comfort and security those old-fashioned nurseries had." The nursery was "a world in miniature, a state within a state." Little Margaret and Elizabeth were capable of falling on each other savagely, in "good old nursery fashion, with no quarter given." As governess, Crawfie was in a senior position to Alah, the nanny, and Bobo, the nursemaid, both of whom stayed in attendance for the rest of their days, as was then the custom. (Nannies were given nicknames by their charges, an upper-class token of affection that was also extended to horses, roommates, and schoolmasters.) Among the book's countless delightful tidbits is the fact that when Philip courted Elizabeth, he did it by having dinner with her, "in the old comfortable nursery fashion, in the nursery. . . . The food was the simplest. Fish, some sort of sweet and orangeade." (This alliance of the erotic and the domestic impulses, typical among the English upper classes, speaks volumes about Prince Charles's enduring attraction to frumpy, comfortable Camilla Parker Bowles, which Americans find so puzzling.)

Who actually wrote this gem? The author's identity

remains a mystery, although he or she was clearly influenced by *Rebecca*, which had been published five years earlier. Both narrators have been granted privileged glimpses into the lives of the aristocracy, and they share the sensitivities of outsiders, cataloguing every china teacup and silver fork, running their fingers over thick damask and silk, taking it all in. The narrators are supernumeraries, literary handmaidens to the main characters, with whom they have become obsessed.

Crawford's life was ruined by the publication of the book, which shouldn't have surprised her. She had written to the queen mother about the possibility of writing it and been told that "people in positions of confidence with us must be utterly oyster. . . . I do feel most strongly that you must resist the allure of American money and persistent editors and say No, No, No to offers of dollars for articles about something as private and precious as our family." Chillingly the letter also avowed, "You would lose all your friends, because such a thing has never been done or even contemplated amongst the people who serve us so loyally."

After the first set of galleys was printed and read by the royal family, Crawford was cut off, never again speaking to the children she had raised. She lived out her days in despair, returning to her native Scotland and using some of her royalties to buy a cottage located on the very road that the royal family traveled on their frequent trips to

Balmoral. She attempted suicide twice, with one of her notes reading, "I cannot bear for those I love to pass me by on the road."

•   •   •

THE SUCCESS of *The Little Princesses* was sufficient to give publishers the impetus for creating a new mini-genre: the nanny memoir. There was no shortage of former nannies willing to spill the beans for a price; the problem was locating a set of charges who were already the objects of tremendous public affection and whose daily routines were conducted within the framework of historic events of international consequence. So it was not until 1965 that a second such volume was produced. *White House Nanny,* the account of Maud Shaw, who was for seven years nanny to Caroline and John Kennedy, was published three years after their father's assassination, when the national hunger for information about JFK's children had reached a fevered zenith. It, too, was a bestseller.

The books are peas in a pod. The two nannies shared the same childlike reverence for their employers, both were enchanted but not cowed by their charges, and both were utterly convinced of the soundness of their commonsensical approach to child rearing. As with *The Little Princesses,* the publication of *White House Nanny* resulted in heartbreak for its author. For the rest of her life, Shaw's letters to the Kennedy family were returned unopened. She never again saw the two children whom she had raised from birth.

Shaw was born in Malta, worked briefly as a nanny in London, and then moved to the States, hoping to take advantage of the American preference for English governesses. She was delighted to take a position with the handsome young senator and his aristocratic wife. The three of them were made for one another. She treated them with the elaborate formality that the Kennedys pretended to abjure but secretly adored. (She insisted, for example, on calling him Senator Kennedy, because "I believe that if someone has a title it ought to be used.") They treated her with the unerring decency and kindness that aristocrats often reserve for their servants, and less frequently for one another.

For her part Jacqueline Bouvier Kennedy — who had been raised in a houseful of servants, among them formally trained nannies — made it clear that she understood the most important point of pride to a nanny: that she is there to care for the children and no one else. "The whole seven and a half years I was with her," Shaw wrote admiringly, "she never so much as asked me to pick up a pin. Even when we were in the White House, she never once asked me to do anything that wasn't strictly within my province." (In private, however, Jackie's attitude toward the woman was less respectful. In one of the flirtatious notes she wrote to the White House steward, Jim West, she reported that Shaw's needs were simple: "just a bedside table for her dentures and a wastebasket for her banana peels.")

In Shaw's account we see all the great old nanny themes, from her proprietary attitude toward the children ("the cook in Palm Beach was always happy to see my two") to the amazing intimacy of her daily life with her wards: John's and Caroline's bedrooms flanked Shaw's in a suite far from the president's, and she ate all her meals and spent all her waking hours with them, until each began school. The unflappable superiority toward other servants, which is the nanny's prerogative, extended even to the Secret Service agents, whom Shaw treated like so many bumbling footmen, scolding them for spoiling the children. (The book's most moving moment involves those agents. After the president had been shot, they stood outside Miss Shaw's bedroom door and drew lots to decide who would be the one to take the terrible job of telling her, and hence the children, the news.)

The book reveals the amazing scope of Shaw's responsibilities, which included something no contemporary nanny would agree to take on: disciplining the children. Once, when they were on holiday at Glen Ora, the Bouvier estate in Virginia, Caroline wandered away. When she suddenly reappeared, Shaw reacted in a way that today might have landed her in prison, but that in 1965 was the stuff of casual revelation: "I whirled around at the sound of Caroline's voice behind me. And I saw her climbing out of one of the little chicken houses, quite un-concerned. That, I know, was the only time I smacked Caroline without sufficient reason. I was so frightened moments before and now so relieved that I gave her a good hard smack on the bottom."

• • •

THE ENRAPTURED, SENSIBLE, and bottom-smacking Maud Shaw is hard to find in the Kennedy family photos. Whenever the children were in the company of both their parents and the press, Shaw made herself scarce. Many of the most famous photographs, such as John running to his father in the portico of the West Wing, have been tightly cropped to frame their famous subjects. But like the Zelig of domestic service, Shaw is always there, visible (barely) in wider shots, where she is seen lingering behind a column like a ghost or peeking out from behind a bit of shrubbery, or where a flash of her white gabardine uniform is glimpsed just beyond an open door of the Oval Office.

In the history of the world, there has never been a family with a more acute sense of the photographic record they wanted to create of themselves. Jackie, of course, was not only clothes-obsessed and heartbreakingly photogenic, but she also had dabbled in press photography during the years before her marriage. She knew the rules of engagement as well as anyone. The press was complicit in obscuring Shaw's presence because they were as enamored of the narrative the Kennedys had shaped for themselves as was the public: that although the family was graced with all the money and power in the world, they conducted their private lives like any American suburban family. When Jackie and her children strode into frame at a White House event, the three of them dressed to the nines, it presented a fiction that was at the heart of President Kennedy's appeal to many female voters: He was a war hero and a family man. He was like the men they had married. And they were like Jackie, turning out well-behaved children and also taking time to comb their own hair and to put on lipstick before their husbands returned at the end of the day.

It is impossible to imagine books like *The Little Princesses* or *White House Nanny* becoming successes today. The modern female reader is quick to observe that any accomplished mother's worldly achievements are suspect if they have been facilitated by the hard work of a nanny. But the women who made bestsellers of the nanny memoirs were at once more innocent and more sophisticated than modern readers. American women read such accounts partly because they offered intimate glimpses of the luxurious ways of the aristocracy, but also because they were curious to read about the child-rearing practices and tips of these polished, educated experts. Housewives identified with both the mothers and the nannies. They spent part of each day being Jackie Kennedy — attending to the matters of a household, the business of being a wife — and part of each day being Maud Shaw — dressing, feeding, and entertaining small children.

•   •   •

IT WAS IN THE FLUSH of this new interest in the child-rearing practices of the aristocracy, shortly after *The Little Princesses* had become a bestseller, that Walt Disney set his sights on making a movie out of Pamela Travers's Mary Poppins books. His discovery of the novels is part of a firmly held Disney legend, one that begins with his climbing the stairs of his Holmby Hills house one night in the early fifties and hearing such delighted laughter coming from his daughter's room that he knocked on her door to see what she was reading.

Diane Disney was reading *Mary Poppins,* which had been published in 1934 and has remained popular ever since. By that point, Walt Disney had had great success with the classic English children's stories of the Victorian and Edwardian eras, including *Peter Pan, Alice in Wonderland,* and *The Wind in the Willows.* Travers's book, which evoked the same sentiments and world, seemed guaranteed to produce another hit.

As Disney saw it, there were two problems to solve if a movie was to be made about Mary Poppins. First, a coherent narrative structure had to be constructed, because the books are not really novels, but, rather, collections of self-contained short stories, some of which scarcely involve Mary Poppins and the Banks children at all. Second, making the books' basic premise — that an unemployed, married, middle-class mother would engage a nanny to raise her children rather than doing the work herself — comprehensible to postwar readers would be a challenge.

The literary Mary Poppins is by no means an untroubling character. Indeed, at the end of the first chapter of the first book — in which she arrives as a shape hurled against the front door in the midst of a gale, assumes the form of a woman, bullies Mrs. Banks into hiring her, snaps at the children, and doses them with a mysterious potion after she gets them alone in the nursery — she earns only a qualified endorsement: "And although they sometimes found themselves wishing for the quieter, more ordinary days when Katie Nanna ruled the household, everybody, on the whole, was glad of Mary Poppins's arrival." She is, in fact, very often "angry," "threatening," "scornful," and "frightening." She calls the children cannibals, jostles them down the stairs, and makes them eat so quickly that they fear they will choke. She has a habit of saving the children from horrifying supernatural experiences, it's true, but this would seem more of a boon if she herself hadn't brought them on in revenge for naughtiness. Often, she seems like someone who doesn't like children much.

Still, they love her. It is Mary Poppins who puts the children to bed and unbuttons their overcoats and bathes them; Mary Poppins who, familiar to the children simply by her scent — toast and Sunlight soap — comes to their bedsides and comforts them with warm milk and quiet words. It is Mary Poppins who earns the deepest love a child has to offer: that which is bound in his trusting dependence on the person who provides his physical care. "Mary Poppins," Michael cries in anguish the first night she has come to care for them. "You'll never leave us, will you?" It's the great question of childhood, the question upon which all the Mary Poppins books turn: Is the person on whom a child relies for the foundation of his existence — food and warmth and love at its most elemental — about to disappear?

"I'll stay till the wind changes," she tells him honestly, and at the first book's end she leaves abruptly. Mrs. Banks is furious; the children are heartbroken. "Mary Poppins is the only person I want in the world," Michael shrieks, throwing himself on the floor. His outburst would be doubly wounding to the modern mother; her child would be suffering and she would be reminded of the love she had forfeited to an employee. But Mrs. Banks is untroubled by either fact. Her concerns are for the disruption of her household. She and Mr. Banks have a dinner party to attend, and it's the maid's day off.

The story of *Mary Poppins* depended on the premise that it was normal for a middle-class family to employ a staff, including a servant to raise the children. But to a large segment of Disney's intended audience this idea would be bewildering or, at least, cold and unpalatable. To solve this problem, he summoned Richard and Robert Sherman to a meeting in his large corner office on the Disney lot in Burbank. The Sherman brothers were songwriters in their early thirties who had worked on several Disney movies and television shows and had recently written the Annette Funicello hit "Tall Paul." They had impressed Disney with the way they "thought story" when they wrote songs. He asked the brothers a question that is now a part of the lore that surrounds the making of *Mary Poppins*: "Do you boys know what a nanny is?"

"Yeah," Richard joked. "It's a goat."

Disney realized that translating the story for an American audience would require an explanation of the role of a nanny, as well as a plot that would reward Mr. and Mrs. Banks for choosing to bring up their children themselves.

"We had to come up with a need for Mary Poppins to come to the Banks family," Richard Sherman told me. "We had to make her a necessary person."

Their first thought was to get rid of Mr. Banks. "We were going to set the thing during the Boer War and have his regiment called up," he said. "Then you could have had a real happy ending, when he came home." And then, Sherman said, they had an inspiration: "You could make the father *emotionally* absent."

Mr. Banks's journey would provide the narrative arc of the film. The mother would be a matron who had lost sight of her most important calling: raising her children. She, too, would be transformed into a good mother (of the kind recognizable to an American audience in the early nineteen-sixties) through the offices of Mary Poppins, who would leave, never to return, once her work with the parents had been completed. "We made it a story about a dysfunctional family," Sherman said. "And in comes Mary Poppins — this necessary person — to heal them."

The script for *Mary Poppins* is set in London in 1910, in the household of a martinet banker (Mr. Banks), a suffragette (Mrs. Banks), and their two young children, Jane and Michael. But the Bankses' story opens with an entirely contemporary predicament — a mother with tons of work is blindsided by a crisis more terrifying to the maternal soul than infidelity or financial reversal: nanny trouble. When first we meet Mrs. Banks, she is dancing along the pavement outside her house, triumphant in her day's accomplishments. "We had the most glorious meeting," she tells her servants, after she bursts through the front door, singing. "Mrs. Whitbourne-Allen chained herself to the wheel of the Prime Minister's carriage. You should have been there! And Mrs. Ainslie — she was carried off to prison, singing and scattering pamphlets all the way!" The servants, however, have news of their own: the reason that Katie Nanna, the children's nursemaid, is wearing her gabardine traveling outfit is that she is about to quit. They finally manage to tell Mrs. Banks, and it is as though they'd stuck a pin in her; we watch her crumple before our eyes. She snatches off her "Votes for Women" sash — "You know how the cause infuriates Mr. Banks" — and then does what any clear-thinking, intelligent woman in her situation would do: she begs. "Katie Nanna — I beseech you. Please reconsider. Think of the children. Think of Mr. Banks." Speak of the devil — he marches through the door, and becomes apoplectic when he learns of the upheaval. In six minutes of film time, Mrs. Banks is changed from a balls-out feminist — "No more the meek and mild subservients, we!" — to a surrendered wife. "I'm sorry, dear," she says. "I'll try to do better next time."

What follows is the entirety of what most people remember of the film: Mary Poppins alights calmly from the sky, using her umbrella as a parachute, and begins to set things straight. Her main objective is to transform Mr. Banks from a prig to a loving mid-century American-style dad, with a hankering for kiddie fun and family time. But she's got half an eye on the missus. By the movie's end,

Mrs. Banks has abandoned the whole crazy suffrage scheme, and proves it by using her "Votes for Women" sash as a tail for the children's kite. As Mary Poppins slips away, Mrs. Banks goes to the park with her family, embracing her proper role in the household. The story's happy ending depends on a signal fact: the Banks children will no longer be brought up by servants. Henceforth, their own mother — corralled homeward through the beneficent intercessions of Mary Poppins — will do the job herself.

And so Walt Disney accomplished two things in a single movie: introducing the American audience to the wonderful English tradition of the nanny, and then warning them never to get one. It was a warning American mothers would heed for almost thirty years.

That's My Woman

I WAS STANDING in my closet on a Saturday afternoon when I learned that I was pregnant. No surprise, really; I had spent the previous twelve months in a forced march toward the condition, and eventual success was all but assured. The doctor who was on the telephone had been a key player in my campaign, both strategist and infantryman. Now he was giddy in his victory: I wasn't just pregnant. I was going to have twins.

As desperate as I was for a baby, the notion that two fertilized eggs were now burrowing into my delicate and unreliable womb, unfolding according to their own secret logic of expansion and domination, was as frightening as it was exciting.

I had been the kind of little girl who dressed the cats in baby clothes and took them for walks in a doll carriage. I had been the kind of teenager who would rather babysit than go on a date. All my life I had been dreaming of having a baby.

I had never imagined having twins. How could I fall in love with two babies at once? I was going to be like someone at a tennis match — gazing down into one little face and then snapping my head around to gaze at his double. It would be like having two husbands. (Truth be told, I *have* had two husbands. But not at the same time. They were singletons; they were only children.)

I bought a book about twins that showed a mother with two babies suckling at her like piglets latched onto a sow. The women in the twins book seemed to have gone mad with worry and exhaustion before the babies even arrived. Pregnancy had pumped them full of twice the normal amount of crazy-making hormones, caused their bellies to expand so much that the skin cracked, and required them to spend months in bed. Some had been forced to use bedpans, which their husbands delivered and emptied. I had imagined my husband holding out my chair at a fancy restaurant; I had imagined him treating me like a precious and delicate child.

According to the book, after the babies arrived all hell was going to break loose. I'd be gargantuan and overwhelmed. "Accept all offers of help," it said, introducing a word and a concept — *help* — that was about to change my life. The kind of help the book recommended involved soliciting covered dishes from one's church and allowing a close friend to clean your bathrooms once in a while. But in Los Angeles in 1998, the word *help* meant something very different.

For the next eight and a half months the thing most often said to me by other women was, "Are you getting help?" They did not offer to help me themselves, although many of them were generous people. They were eager to shower me with Tiffany rattles and Bellini car coats, and to get my name bumped to the top of the nursery school waiting list. But they never once mentioned casseroles or scouring the bathtub. As far as those things went, I needed to get *help:* someone I paid, not someone to whom I was bound by the complications of friendship and community. Not someone to whom I would someday owe similar intimacies and inconvenience. When we interviewed a popular pediatrician, I discovered that getting help was medically indicated. His nurse took one look at my stupendous girth, put two and two together, and took me aside: "Re-fi the house if you have to," she said. "Just get help."

I once spent a week with a woman who had a large house in London, two small sons, and more cheerful housekeepers and nannies than you could count. I would have loved to be at the helm of a household like that, spending mornings in my dressing gown bouncing the baby on my knee and chatting companionably with my cheery staff until I put on something smart and went out to lunch, leaving the ladies behind to run loads of laundry and polish the wooden end tables and put the pasha down for his nap. The problem was, we were not in an ideal situation to begin employing servants. To begin with, we had no house to "re-fi." We were living in the top half of a duplex with an efficiency kitchen and no washer and dryer. Two years earlier I had quit my teaching job to become a writer, which had turned out to be a humiliating bust. Whatever my relationship with the help was going to be, it certainly wasn't going to be modeled on the matrons of South Kensington.

What would ultimately vex and trouble my relationship with the nanny, however, was not my financial straits. It was that as much as I had dreamed and planned and hoped for a baby, I was unprepared for the way that motherhood would transform me.

●   ●   ●

THE NIGHT THE TWINS WERE BORN, I had what I can only describe as a conversion experience. I didn't want to be the person I was anymore. I didn't want to be funny or outrageous or careless. I didn't want to be the girl who always needed to be bailed out of things, or the one

whose helplessness was among her most attractive qualities. I wanted to reinvent myself. It had already happened:
the moment Rob carried the babies, one at a time, to the
top of the operating table so that I could get a good look
at them, a door swung shut behind me. A thousand possibilities were sealed behind it: all the possibilities of my
girlhood had come to an end. And I couldn't have cared
less. *This* was what I wanted to do.

For the first time in my life I was gripped by a sense of
purpose. I had spent my whole life waiting for one. I had
always felt myself to be a person charged with ambition
and talent and drive, but these qualities had always been
free-floating, never attaching themselves to any certain
goal. As a girl I had imagined some sort of television
career for myself. As a young woman art history had
seemed to be the answer. But I had no sooner stacked a
pile of monographs on the quattrocento painters in my
study carrel than a profound sleepiness descended upon
me. For two years I couldn't quite wake up. I made plans
to quit the program almost as soon as I'd begun it. In my
early thirties I'd been seized by the conviction that I
should become a novelist (I knew just the crisp white shirt
to wear for the dust jacket photograph), and I'd even quit
a good teaching job to bang out the necessary text. I
typed away for a year, but then things slowed down considerably, and then stopped altogether. In a matter of a
few months, I became a young woman with no job and

no hope of getting one. Going back to teaching was unthinkable after FLANAGAN LEAVING TO WRITE NOVEL had been a headline in the school newspaper.

A pregnancy would have been face-saving, but that seemed as difficult to come by as a brilliant first novel. The two became one in my mind: no baby, no book. It seemed I couldn't go anywhere without someone asking either, "How's the novel coming along?" or "Any plans for a baby?" Worst of all was the unintentionally precise, cheerfully delivered observation that "right now, your book is your baby!" I was defined by failure, a person who was stuck, who could produce neither book (a common predicament, if embarrassing) nor baby (a failure of womanhood itself, the one area at which I had always excelled).

But then, on an operating table in Santa Monica Hospital, all the old failures and self-recriminations came to an immediate halt. Giving birth was the most surprising thing that had ever happened to me. On some deep psychic level I hadn't really believed the pregnancy was ever going to end. I'd thought it was going to be like the novel — lots and lots of typing, an ever-growing accumulation of "product," but no final result. At the baby shower we'd had a pool for when the babies would arrive, and one by one I'd crossed off the losing guesses — until there were none left. The latest guess was February 2; that came and went, and still I was pregnant: pregnancy block.

And then everything changed on a dime. We went to the weekly checkup, had the sonogram, and spent half an hour in a booth while I sat on a La-Z-Boy with two seat belts strapped around my planet-size tummy, measuring uterine contractions. The doctor read the tape and made a pronouncement: I was to report to the hospital at once. The babies had chosen their moment. We had to cut them off at the pass with a cesarean section, or there would be hell to pay.

An epidural (frightening and painful), an operating room (filled with masked strangers and dominated by a dry-erase board on which were written the words SHARPS COUNT), and then the sensation of being cut open — a great tugging and pushing and as much physical terror as I've ever known. The tugging assumed a brute force, there was a shoving jolt, and then something vital was wrenched out of me. For a measureless piece of time, nothing at all happened. Not a sound or a movement.

Then — pandemonium.

There were cheers and congratulations. Even the dour anesthesiologist popped off his stool to take a curious look over the blue drape that shielded me from my future.

And then — of all things! at a time like this! — there was the unmistakable sound of a baby crying.

"Caitlin, here he is . . ."

Over the curtain, held in gloved hands, gray and furious — a baby.

A human baby.

I couldn't have been more shocked if she'd held up a toaster or a bicycle tire. It was the word made flesh. *Pregnant* had been transformed into a baby.

And then more tugging, more cheering, my husband reduced to astonished laughter — another one!

The Apgar scores were perfect. The weights were remarkable. We had chosen Santa Monica Hospital because of its famous neonatal intensive care unit, but there was no need for it.

I had, at long last, done something right.

We spent four days in the hospital, marveling over the babies and being tended by a phalanx of medical people, which seemed entirely appropriate. The babies were starter scraps of humanity; constant vigilance was in order. The hospital seemed to have adopted my own gathering paranoia and taken it one step further. On the babies' scrawny legs were enormous security sensors: if anyone tried to take them beyond the confines of the maternity ward, the entire hospital would go on lockdown. There wasn't just the babies' frailty to worry about; there was their beauty. Someone would want them; everyone would want them. We would have to be on guard.

The doctor stopped by and marveled over their perfection. It must have been a stock speech, but I took it hook, line, and sinker. The other babies in the nursery were gormless and common; some were ugly. Ours were trailing clouds of glory. They would look off to the corner of the hospital room and smile; they were still in communication with the place they had come from.

Just when I had become accustomed to the hospital's benign routines — the trays of bland food, the mind-softening painkillers, the washcloth baths — we were turfed out. The vigilance had ended. A clerk with a great sheaf of papers came into the room, and we signed and initialed forms; accepted glossy brochures and free products (everything in duplicate, of course); and signed releases of liability. It was like buying a car. We were about to drive them off the showroom floor.

Rob was sent off for the wheelchair, and I was left alone with the babies and my first task: dressing them for the trip home. I took out of my suitcase the little matching sleepers I had bought weeks earlier — folding and refolding them like dolls' clothes, imagining this very moment — and carefully maneuvered Patrick into one. He peed all over it (loose diaper), and a nurse stopped by and clucked at my ineptitude.

The babies and I were brought to the front door of the hospital, where the green Volvo (chosen with this very moment in mind) was waiting. In a matter of minutes we left the walled city. For the first time the four of us were alone. Not a family yet, just two stunned adults and two infants, who clearly ought to spend another few months incubating and pulling themselves together. The short drive back to the apartment was harrowing. The car seats faced backward: how were we to be sure the babies weren't strangling or suffocating? We stopped several times, talking tensely to each other, to check on them.

Waiting on the front steps of our duplex was the baby nurse I had hired. For a heartrending sum of money she was going to provide our babies with the very best care. She drove me crazy before she'd climbed to the top of the stairs. She was officious, imperious, lonely, and, worst of all, loquacious. I fired her the next morning, over the telephone, as I did her replacement, who was no better.

I felt strong, confident, and entirely sure of myself when I fired the baby nurses. They were educated white women like me; I had hired them through a reputable service. I knew what I was doing. Besides, our real help — our nanny — was on her way. Things would soon settle down to normal.

It would take two years before I fully understood that what I considered my normal life had ended.

•   •   •

ONE OF MY FRIENDS who had recommended hiring a nanny had referred to the employee as being "a second pair of arms," which was a very comforting notion. Disembodied, she would be nothing more than two helpful appendages, changing a diaper or running a load of laundry. She would be no more of a human presence in the household than the useful refrigerator, the attractive white changing table. She would shadow me as I worked.

In fact her actual presence in the household — her spirit, her easy affection, her countless kindnesses, her exasperating stubbornness of habit — would transform it. And my relationship with her would turn out to be the most legally, morally, and emotionally complicated one of my life.

●　　　●　　　●

I SHOULD EXPLAIN: I am not someone who is troubled, for political or personal reasons, by the idea of hiring people to work in my household.

For example, we have a gardener now (we've come up in the world since the days of the efficiency kitchen), and he and I do not have an intimate or a troubling relationship. He's been working here for two years, and I don't even know his last name.

What I know about him is this: he is Central American; he has crooked teeth; he laughs a lot. He shows up when he is supposed to, which is why I have not fired him, as I did his predecessor. Sometimes I think his bill is high, but I never complain.

We seem to have a friendly enough relationship, although I'm sure he has slotted me into such broad categories — white woman, cheerful, rich but stingy about planting too many annuals — that I am unknowable to him. I've done the same to him: immigrant, hard worker, a kidder but perhaps a bit of a tyrant to his truckful of day workers.

We have never quarreled. We have never had a glass of wine together. We have never discussed our marriages or, however obliquely, our sex lives. We have never lavished expensive gifts on each other, or complained bitterly about each other to our friends, or gone on holiday together. I have never spoken sharply to him and made him cry. I have never felt paralyzed in his absence, or dreamed about him, or heard my children call out for him in the night. He has never seen me naked or weeping; he has never nursed me through an illness. I have never lent him money and then immediately excused the debt, or given an imperious bureaucrat a dressing-down on his behalf, or had long meetings with his son's Head Start teacher, or paid for another of his children to attend summer school, or asked him to clean a toilet when one of my own children has sullied it.

In short, there has never been any possible context in which we might begin, however tentatively, to breach the inexpressively vast gulf of culture, language, history, and fortune that separates us.

On the other hand — my nanny.

Or am I to say, on the English model, "my children's nanny"? (You see: already things have gotten complicated.)

Paloma.

Linda — that's her nickname, although almost no one here, in America, knows it. That's what I call her when I want to make her laugh, or when I'm scolding her for working too hard: Linda.

The scar on her right arm is from a cat. Her left ring finger is missing the tip because a door slammed on it. (She was three; her mother was at work, and her sister Lita was minding her.)

She used to weigh 116 pounds! It makes us laugh to think of it. But I've seen the photographs; it's true.

I know about her daughter, the first one, the baby who died.

I know about the time when she was a teenager in Honduras and two policemen told her to get in their car. She was certain she was going to be raped, but then a miracle happened: an uncle of hers happened upon the scene. He knew one of the policemen, and he convinced the man to let her out. I know how she felt when the car door swung open again and a wedge of light fell across her, and her uncle reached in to help her climb out onto the bright pavement.

She knows more of the details about my first wedding — the yellow-and-white-striped tent, the fresh flowers woven into my hair, the gift of my mother's pearls — than anyone who was in attendance, and she knows that my first husband came from a rich family. But to this day she can't understand why I left him. The notions of incompatibility and youthful misjudgment that I have tendered baffle her. Why would I leave a rich man?

In our own way, we loved each other. Still, I was the boss.

"Paloma, Patrick is throwing up!" I would tell her, and she would literally run to his room, clean the sheets, change his pajamas, spread a clean towel on his pillow, feed him ice chips, sing to him. I would stand in the doorway, concerned, making funny faces at Patrick to cheer him up — the way my father did when I was sick and my mother was taking care of me.

I wanted Paloma to be my friend and equal, but I also wanted her to do what I told her. Most of the time she did.

●　　　●　　　●

HOW DID I FIND HER? It was easy. The city is full of them. If you want to find a contractor who will remodel your kitchen sometime before the next presidential election without disappearing for weeks on end midway through the job or cracking the unsealed Italian marble you special-ordered from a catalogue, good luck to you.

But if you want someone to take charge of your children, you can take your pick, and they can all start tomorrow.

Paloma and I were both on the rebound — wounded and wary after bad breakups — when we got together. My first nanny, who was called Marta, had been lured back by her previous employers. They wooed her away from me with a fat raise and brought something to the bargaining table that ended negotiations before they began: they lived close to her, and they promised to drive her home each day.

Her last week was terrible. I was filled with doom and abandonment. Was it her former charge — the formidable and much-discussed Penelope, age three, for whom I had developed a pure hatred — who was enticing her back, not the raise or the easy commute? Maybe she was rejecting us, the babies and me. Maybe she didn't love us enough.

Two nannies came and left in short order. First there was a Filipina, who was newly arrived to these shores and single-mindedly dedicated to producing very white socks. She would make a brew of bleach and Tide in a bucket, mix in the babies' tiny socks, and then leave the concoction in the sunlight on the back porch for a few hours, stirring it as faithfully as a roux. She left one day and never came back. Next there was a Honduran woman, very nice and quite formally dressed, who believed our most pressing household problem was an absence of freshly cooked food. She would leave the babies to me, ignore the unmade beds and the chaotic living room, and install herself in our tiny kitchen, cooking. I came to dread the scratch of her key in the lock because I was always promising, and never managing, to have procured the ingredients she needed: ground beef, onions, potatoes. Her disappointment was hard to endure. She assessed us as a hopeless case. After a couple of weeks she said that she'd decided to become a seamstress, specializing in wedding and *quinceanera* dresses. (The details of the plan changed all the time, although its intent — to extricate herself from our chaotic lives — was always clear.) That was the last we saw of her.

Paloma had been happily taking care of a little girl named Claire, who had been in her care since birth, three years earlier. But there had been an incident of some kind between Paloma and Claire's mother. ("She yell me," Paloma finally admitted, still angry and shamed many months later.) Pride had forced her to quit without having anything else lined up.

She arrived at our apartment on a particularly hectic Sunday morning. I had forgotten she was coming; I didn't remember scheduling the meeting or even talking to her on the telephone. Later this would seem magical, as though she had arrived via the same calling that had summoned Mary Poppins. I let her in the door; she reached for Conor in his high chair, causing him to wriggle and flirt, and agreed to Marta's old rate. We were in business.

•   •   •

AND SO THE STAGE WAS SET for the development of a particular and ancient type of relationship: that of a woman and the servant who cares for her children.

Once, after Paloma had left our employ, I asked her whom the babies had loved more, her or me. She replied with quick conviction, "*You*, Mrs. Kate!"

I reminded her of the time Patrick had reached for her instead of for me after a nap.

"Oh, that's because he was a *baby!*" she said, half in Spanish, half in English. "He was confused."

Confused about what?

"He knew I was changing the diaper and feeding the bottle, and he thought, *That's my woman.* But then he got older, and he learned! He knew! He looked at you and he thought, *Oh, no — that's my woman!*"

•   •   •

NANNY-MOTHER RELATIONSHIPS come in two varieties, the first of which occurs when the mother works outside the home. The employee arrives just as the mother is leaving for work in the morning and departs the moment her employer returns. These relationships exist largely in the abstract, forged of notes and telephone calls and the odd morning when the mother works from home. In a typical week the mother and nanny may spend less than an hour in each other's company. This sounds like a straightforward relationship, but in my experience many working mothers spend so much time fretting about the child's divided allegiance that they are torn between wild gratitude to the nanny for providing love when the mother cannot, and extreme anxiety that the child is getting confused about which woman is the mother — which, if the child is young enough, he probably is.

I have often thought that the American preoccupation with rooting out cruel and unfeeling nannies — buying video cameras sewn into teddy bears, doubling back to the house to peer into windows, and so on — is really a somewhat hysterical reaction to the possibility of the opposite: nannies who share pure and wholly reciprocated love with their charges. This is dangerous territory for all concerned. On the one hand, if the mother is called out of town for a day or two (as I was for both of my parents' deaths and once — how thrilling! how important I felt! — for work), is there any more blessed and calming sensation than knowing that your child is in the hands of someone who knows and loves him almost as much as you do? On the other hand, because the mother relinquishes so much to the nanny, she often possesses a quietly burning antipathy toward the woman. Sometimes ending the relationship is the only way to assert control over what is happening at home. Is it any wonder that so many nanny jobs end in blowups and abrupt sackings?

The second type of relationship, when mother and nanny work side by side, is more intimate, more vexing, more rewarding, and more emotionally complicated. In such cases relationships of exquisite intensity almost always result — even when mistress and caregiver are not employer and employee. In Eugene Genovese's great study of American slavery, *Roll, Jordan, Roll,* he observes:

> The black and white women of the Big House needed each other. They lived as part of a single family, although by no means always a happy, peaceful, or loving one. If black mammies and nurses usually delivered the white babies, white mistresses sometimes delivered the black and more often helped look after both mother and infant. If mammies and nurses raised the white children, mistresses helped raise the black, so that the children, white and black, were constantly underfoot and a joy and a trial to all. Mistresses with drunken, dissolute, spendthrift, or brutal husbands poured out their troubles to their maids, who poured out

their own troubles to their mistresses and to each other. If a woman, white or black, woke up at night terrified by a dream of impending death, she would run to her maid or her mistress for comfort.

One does not want to compare oneself to a slaveholder — and certainly not when one is paying a handsome rate, chipping in for a new car, and never docking pay for absences or lateness — but that description sounds more like my relationship with Paloma than anything else I've come across. Her two sons, ages three and six when she began working for us, were often in the apartment. The bewilderment that I felt about feeding schedules and colic, Paloma felt about the American educational system. Within a month of her starting with us, I was attending the open house at her son's school. I would gladly leave the confinement of the apartment to pick up her other son from nursery school, where I would occasionally have long discussions about his progress with the cheerful supervisor. The boy would come home with me, sprawl across the big chair in the living room, and take a nap. Paloma began to look at me with new regard. She had loved my babies from the start, but once I started helping out with her children, we entered new waters; our relationship was transformed. We were bound together in the deep way of women: through our shared love of each other's children.

Sometimes on Friday afternoons I would press a glass of wine on her, and we would stand around the kitchen, laughing and drinking together, like a debauched pair from a Hogarth print: *The Slatternly Housewife, and Her Maid*.

No man is a hero to his valet. Still, I think she loved me. I know I loved her.

•   •   •

ALL OF MY FRIENDS seemed to be developing similar relationships with their nannies: the same overwhelming sense of love and gratitude, the same intimacy, the same moments of insecurity and shame that we weren't doing all of the baths or the breakfasts ourselves.

People talked about their nannies with an intensity usually reserved for love affairs. The nanny was amazing; she was — invariably and almost instantly — "a member of the family." One friend raced out to Nordstrom to buy her nanny a leather jacket as a gift for handling a minor household crisis so well. Another told her nanny chapter and verse about her affair. To hear us talk about our nannies was to sense that a new kind of relationship was being forged in the houses and condominiums of Los Angeles, that in thirty years' time these nannies would still be part of their employers' households, beloved ancients sitting in rocking chairs and waiting for their grown charges to return on holiday.

But then I might run into one of these mothers six months later, and when the nanny's name came up, it was clear that there had been a cooling: "She didn't work out." Often there had been a blowup of some kind, or the nanny had quit over the phone, never to be seen again. Sometimes a discovery had been made — the nanny was sneaking her own laundry into the house, for example, or she had taken the baby to a park or shop that was off-limits — and when the mother had tried to discuss it, there had been an explosive fight. The nannies were mystified by their employers — who could tell what would upset these crazy white women, so generous one moment, so angry the next? Partly, the troubles were the result of the tensions that underlie any love triangle. Whenever a nanny quit without giving notice (nannies rarely gave notice), the employer would be furious that the nanny had cut her ties with a child who loved her so much. Everyone was eager for kindergarten, when nannies could be taken out of the equation altogether.

It seemed that a nanny relationship was like a love affair: born out of the most urgent needs, quick to flame, and just as quick to burn out.

●　　●　　●

IN MY CASE the tensions did not evolve from laundry disputes or cheapness. The problem was the collision of my conversion experience and the rude discovery that I was impressively unsuited to my new vocation. It was like being a chubby ballerina or a clumsy surgeon. I couldn't get those babies to do a single thing the books described — and I had read a library full of them.

I knew the steps for creating a "Baby Wise" baby, a "Ferberized" baby, or a Penelope Leach "settled" baby. I understood Dr. Spock's philosophy, which required me to take a hero's journey, looking deep into myself and discovering that I was already in possession of everything I was going to need. (The book itself was apparently a seven-hundred-page appendix to my untapped native wisdom.) I had read T. Berry Brazelton's famous book *Touchpoints,* which assumed I would develop a schoolgirl's crush on my pediatrician (I was all for it) and also suggested that I encourage the Babkin reflex (thumb sucking). I understood the rationale behind Dr. Sears's weird recommendation that we should all bunk down in the same bed like dingoes in a den, and I knew from La Leche League (a group whose fixation on other women's breasts I came to regard as sexually suspect) that a breast-fed baby would be superior in every possible way to a bottle-fed one. I read these books faithfully during my pregnancy, with the general intention of picking and choosing the bits I liked best, just as on a trip to France one turns to Michelin for some things and to *Let's Go: Paris* for others.

The problem was twofold. In the first place, all of these systems worked only when applied with a draconian singleness of purpose; none allowed for compromise. Second, and more pressing, the babies hadn't read a single one of those books. Neither had Paloma. The three of them got along together like a house on fire. She would no sooner leave a baby to "cry it out" in his crib (as several of the books demanded) than she would put him on an ice floe. She rocked the babies to sleep, singing to them. She wasn't worried that if she showed them how to use a rattle properly or make a squeak toy squeak, she was going to stunt their natural curiosity and self-esteem (as the RIE method made so fearfully clear). She played with them for hours on end, and they loved it. She didn't follow charts and guidelines about when and how to introduce solid food. She arrived one morning with a freshly killed chicken and made soup; the babies lapped it up. She did Dr. Spock one better. Whereas his book begins, "Trust yourself. You know more than you think you do," she apparently knew more than Dr. Spock.

The more I ceded the boys' routine and schedule to Paloma, the happier they were, and the calmer and more livable the household became. But then — the road to Damascus and all — I became a supernumerary in my own conversion experience. Sometimes I would walk into the living room, after taking a walk or going to the supermarket, and discover the three of them in a state of perfect contentment, taking plastic blocks out of a basket or looking at a picture book. The boys would blink up at me as though trying to place my face, and Paloma — who knew that jobs were lost over this kind of moment — would stare at me guiltily, as though caught in flagrante.

That I knew my boys would love her is why I hired her. That they did was unnerving me to the core.

•   •   •

LIKE ALL GOOD MOTHERS, Paloma could transform a household with her presence. Without her the days were shaped by weariness and claustrophobia and isolation. One hour seemed to last ten — unless it was an hour during which both babies were asleep, in which case it seemed to fly past in five minutes. The nonstop rounds of feeding and diapering and rocking them to sleep left no time for anything else. When Paloma wasn't in the apartment, the place immediately became a pigsty — too small, too messy, too shabby. I sometimes imagined that a tornado was constantly whipping through the living room because nothing ever stayed put. A pair of sunglasses set down on the bookcase would instantly vanish, only to turn up a week later wedged deep between the sofa cushions. Keys simply had to be held on to; putting them on any flat surface was as good as throwing them off a cliff. For someone who has a convert's piety about tidiness and order, the experience was unhinging.

But when Paloma was there, the place seemed jolly and cozy, snug and just right. Her presence was immediately and delightfully transformative. She imposed order and routines on the day, which gave them shape and made time resume its old form: each hour composed of sixty evenly proportioned minutes, each of which ticked by in a fulsome and predictable manner. As soon as she arrived in the morning, she would chuck the babies under the chin and murmur to them with obvious fondness, then tidy up the living room — the effect of which was so psychically calming that I would sit down in it and begin to feel the tornado slow. She would change the babies and give them a bottle, and then magically, without a moment's fuss or sorrow, they would drop off into a sleep so deep and perfect it seemed as though they were under anesthesia. She would slip them one after the other into their cribs, and then the delicious, contented peacefulness that occurs when two babies are sleeping at the same time would descend sweetly over the apartment. I might make a cup of tea. I might sit silently in the living room for the length of the nap, like someone stunned after an accident or a trauma.

By the end of the nap I might have regained enough composure to get dressed.

What I did not do was leave. This now seems silly to me, and possibly pathological. Clearly the two things I needed to do during that challenging time of life was to get some more sleep and to cheer up a bit — the second goal best achieved by getting out of the little fortress and creating a private, adult life for myself for a few hours each day. Fifty years ago a young matron in my situation — one lucky enough to have both household help and no need to make money — would have been up and dressed and off to the department store or the library guild or the dry cleaner by midmorning, and no one would have questioned her inclinations as far as motherhood was concerned. But these are very different times, ones fraught with forty years of female advance and retreat, from children toward careers, and then back again. I had chosen to stay home, ensuring that my perfect babies, my life's great achievement, were being made ever more perfect by the fact that their mother was there every day. I didn't have a novel to show for myself — or a set of smart clothes, or my old humor and energy — but I had two babies glowing with mother love.

But then — Paloma.

Could I take all the credit for how brilliantly they were turning out if they were actually in a nanny's care for eight

hours a day? Would I still be the one *raising* the babies —
what an unsettling word — if I was out and about for so
many hours? Every magazine and book on the subject of
being a mother tells you that motherhood can be rede-
fined, that there are all sorts of ways to be a good mother:
a working woman can be just as good a mother as a woman
who stays at home; an unhappy at-home mother can
be quickly transformed — via paid work — into a much-
improved one, her good humor making up for the hours
she is away.

The trouble was, I'd had an excellent mother, so I
knew a few things. A mother took care of her own baby.
She rocked him, sang to him, nursed him through ill-
nesses. She didn't hand off any of those tasks to anyone
else. She wouldn't. When her baby woke from his nap, he
would have no question as to whose face he would soon
see rising godlike above the crib rail: it would always be
his mother's. When he dreamed his baby dreams — of
milk and lullabies and the big flowered chair where he was
fed — he would not be dreaming about a woman his parents had hired; he would be dreaming about his mother.

What I needed to do was stay put, exert my presence,
make sure my beloved sons were imbibing as much of me
as they were of her. I ended up with the worst of both
worlds. Exhausted and ragged, I would mope around beside Paloma all day, watching her do everything with competence and good humor, and then — exhausted, and with

hours to go before they slept again — I would take over the next shifts, during which my inability to keep house and my even more pronounced inability to be upbeat would be thrown into sharper relief by the previous eight hours of domestic consistency.

I grew up unsuccessfully asserting my independence against my mother, and now it was the same with Paloma. I couldn't imagine carrying on without her.

* * *

PALOMA WORKED from nine to five — a span dictated by our finances, not the number of hours she was willing to work — and for a long time the babies woke up at five every morning. All my life I've been a morning person, but during that year I faced the day with a foggy brain, a desperation for sleep, and an emotional weariness that I recognized as depression only many years later. For a four-hour stretch we would sit in the little living room, waiting for Paloma.

First things first: I would switch on MSNBC, feed and change the babies, and put on the teakettle. At last the *Today* show would begin. I would watch it straight through and with an intensity of which its producers could only have dreamed. I assumed at first that I had developed a newfound interest in cooking tips and money management and the weather. But gradually I came to understand that what I liked was seeing people up and dressed and doing their jobs. Even the crowd outside the studio — a group I had once observed with curiosity from a Manhattan coffee shop, wondering what in the world would inspire anyone to show up for such an exercise — now seemed like industrious, happy people: bundled into parkas, radiating good cheer, ready for a jam-packed day of sightseeing. They had important roles to fill in the early hours: they were New York tourists. They didn't want to miss a thing. Back in the apartment, midway through what the hosts called "the seven-o'clock hour," a weak light would begin to fill the living room, illuminating the stains on the carpet. Sometimes I realized we had to get out of there.

Staging the prison break — something Paloma achieved twice a day, always without a moment's trepidation — was arduous. I had to get myself dressed and then get the boys dressed. Immediately one of them would need a clean diaper or drop off into a deep, unscheduled sleep, throwing the whole enterprise into question: maybe his brother would fall asleep, too, and then I could sleep? Many such missions were aborted on this hope, always unrealized. If we pushed on, I would race down the stairs to the porch and set up the double stroller, frantic with anxiety: were the unattended babies turning on the stove or diving headfirst into the toilet? Then I would race up and get one boy, bring him to the stroller and strap him in, race up for his brother (more anxiety: was the boy on the porch being set upon by pit bulls or kidnappers?), and get him squared away in the stroller.

And then — suddenly — we were free.

On our own, out of the terrible apartment. We were like the *Today* show tourists: up and dressed and eager for adventure. The very second I wheeled the huge stroller around and headed down the path toward the sidewalk, I would begin to cheer up. The oppressive apartment, the yammer and glow of the television, were behind us. In my memory of the time it was always winter, cold and fogged in. Buses would rumble past us bearing people to work; the elementary school down the street would be stirring to life. The morning runners would pound past emitting tinny blasts of music from their Walkmans. All would command our curious attention. The school's crossing guard would be just coming on duty, and she became an admirer of the babies. She would make a show of stopping traffic with particular fierceness so that we could cross in state.

We would go to the playground, where we would be the only people because it was so early. I would lift one boy and then the other into the baby swings and swing them a bit, and they would laugh and drool; they loved the swings. It was as though we were the only three people in the world — not an especially comforting thought, but at least we were out of the living room. Once, when we were playing in the deserted playground, one of the babies vanished. I had turned my back to put his brother in a swing, and when I looked back, he had disappeared into the chill white air. What he had done was crawl into the storage bin underneath the stroller, but it took a minute for me to think of looking there, and I ran around the playground unsure whether I was up against human or supernatural forces. Once I had him back — he was grinning in the welter of Cheerios and crumpled napkins — I fell upon him like the Prodigal's father, breathing in the warm solidity of his body through his fleece sweater, resting my teary cheek on his smooth, plump one. I loved him so much; I loved both of them. That love, its intensity and its singular nature, was the compensation for my loneliness and exhaustion.

At last it would be nine o'clock, and I could wheel the mammoth stroller around and head for home. It was the most reassuring feeling in the world to know that Paloma was inside, that order was already being imposed, that the babies would be lifted from me. I felt, as I got closer to the duplex, the way I used to feel when I walked home from school, knowing that my mother was inside the house — that it wasn't a cold, empty structure, that it was humming with comforts and company and safety.

I would ring the bell from the bottom of the steps, and she would come hurrying down them, as though she had been waiting impatiently for us, as though she was eager for the work to begin.

"Rest! Rest!" she would tell me, gesturing at the stairs, letting me know it was okay for me not to help with getting the babies and the stroller inside.

Whenever I went to the park without her, she would reprove me — "That's too hard for you, Mrs. Kate!" — and I would walk up the stone steps to the sound of her clucking over the babies, proprietary and proud.

• • •

I WAS BECOMING quite the Latinophile! No more for me the high school struggle with French, the college assault on Italian. I was learning Spanish the no-pain way: an immersion program. We jabbered away at each other, arriving at the occasional impasse but forging ahead with the help of a hardbound Spanish-English dictionary that Paloma brought from home and kept in a kitchen drawer with the yellow pages. My old copy of *Speedy Spanish for the Maid,* which my first husband had picked up at the supermarket the day we arrived in Los Angeles, was entirely unsuited to the things Paloma and I wanted to discuss. We didn't want to talk about washing the baseboards or leaving a key under the doormat. We wanted to talk about whether or not birth control pills caused infertility, about the war in El Salvador, and about Miss Clairol Leave-In Conditioner. We wanted to talk about the swimming medals Paloma had won before she'd quit school and about the afternoon job she'd held at the age of ten. We wanted to talk about my college years in the South, when bales of snowy sheets and towels were delivered to the dorms each Monday, and the dining hall chef made omelets to order, and my mother sent money for a new ball gown each spring.

In Paloma's care I ate Honduran food and increasingly subscribed to the Honduran method of child rearing, which seemed to depend on a sort of Huey Long approach: every boy a king. Paloma and I indulged the children, fussed over them, arrived in state for pediatrician appointments and haircuts and studio portraits. Anytime I tried to impose an American child-rearing approach — limiting sweets, say, or confiscating a favorite toy as punishment — she would look at me with a baleful, pained expression, and I would cave in immediately. She secretly defied many of my instructions about the children (it was this defiance that was the cause of the two barn-burning fights of our association), and she brazenly defied all the ones that kept her from coddling the boys. It was easier to go along than to fight her, so that's how things were. "It's Paloma's house, and we just live in it," I used to say, mostly with fondness. I didn't want to run the household. I wanted to live in it the way I had once lived in my mother's house:

lightly and with ease, sleeping on fresh sheets and eating good meals and not having to account for how those things came into existence. I didn't have the mind or the patience for housekeeping. I am not an orderly or organized person, and with Paloma I didn't have to be. With her in the house I could play with the babies and write magazine articles and take the boys on excursions.

●　　　●　　　●

TIME WENT BY, and I showered Paloma with treats and surprises, the more whimsical and unexpected the better. One day we were sitting in a McDonald's Playland on a gray, rainy day, and a woman approached us with an Avon catalogue. Paloma admired a photograph of a china doll dressed in an elaborate wedding gown. On the spot I ordered it for her. I liked to give her things.

What I did not give her were Social Security setasides. My understanding of that thorny and bewildering topic came from the famous Senate hearings regarding President Bill Clinton's nomination of Zoe Baird for U.S. attorney general (who withdrew after admitting that she had not paid Social Security for a housekeeper who was an illegal alien). It wasn't anything that applied to me. I wasn't going before Congress. I just needed a little help around the house.

To calculate the rate I was going to pay, I used a formula as old as the marketplace: what was the least amount
I could pay to get the kind of worker I wanted? I offered
Paloma a wage based not on what I could afford or what I
thought the work was worth, but, rather, on what other
women were offering. And she took it — end of story.

But as the months passed, and as my love for Paloma
expanded into something akin to my love for my own
mother (who died midway through Paloma's tenure, cleav-
ing me to Paloma with renewed intensity), I began to ex-
amine more critically the terms of the relationship I had
established with her. They were unlike those any employer
had ever forged with me. On the one hand, I didn't give
her health insurance, make Social Security set-asides, or
pay for workers' compensation. On the other hand, I did
things for her that no "real" job ever would. I gave her
extra money when she needed it, bought her presents,
encouraged her to bring her children to work whenever
she wanted, and took her to medical appointments,
demanding that she receive good care. Our professional
relationship, I vaguely assumed, was that of an independent
contractor (Paloma) and the purchaser of a service (me).

But I was not morally in the clear, as it turned out. In
fact I was complicit in a shameful activity, a cog in the
wheel of several terrible machines. In the course of the
most painful examination of conscience and character that
I have ever made, I realized that our arrangement — so

blessedly beneficial to me, so seemingly propitious for Paloma — was leaving her unprepared for retirement and exposing her children to the threat of poverty if she died. It was also contributing to the erosion of the city I live in and implicating me in the murderous process by which human cargo is transported into this country to ease the lives of the middle class.

This moral crisis began, curiously enough, when I accompanied a friend to a scary place: an oncologist's office. We sat down in the waiting room and immediately noticed that along with the cheery women's magazines and brochures on new medications, there was a tall stack of booklets about Social Security. This seemed an improbable location for such information; it was like finding a DMV form at the hairdresser's. Still, the office seemed eager to disseminate it; the corridor leading to the examining rooms had a rack full of the brochures.

I'll read anything; I read one of the brochures.

And then I realized what I was doing to Paloma.

My previous experience with Social Security had been this: noting that a tiny portion of my paycheck was siphoned off to it, and having my mother offer, shortly before her death, to give me all of her accumulated Social Security dollars (she'd been proudly saving them up in a special account) so that I could join a tennis club.

But reading that brochure, I realized that Social Security isn't a little extra check to sweeten the retirement of well-married ladies. It's the whole game plan for a lot of people: retirement, disability insurance, a plan to support the worker's children if the worker dies. The prose was simple enough for a fifth grader to comprehend, but its effect on me was unlike that of anything I'd ever read. Every worker needs forty credits to qualify; you earn a credit a quarter; in ten years you're eligible for benefits. I left the office with the terrible knowledge that I was doing a shameful thing.

Friends, all of whom were doing exactly what I was doing, rushed to assuage my guilt. Who knew if Social Security would even be around by the time Paloma retired? It was better, they said, to put a little money aside each month in a money market account and tell her not to touch it until she was sixty-five. I supposed that was true — although none of my friends was doing such a laudable thing. And besides, we were all liberals. Weren't we supposed to be violently opposed to privatizing Social Security?

My old ace in the hole — the notion that Paloma was an independent contractor — turned out to be bogus. The federal tax code makes it explicitly clear that domestic workers are not, under any circumstances, independent contractors. They are always employees. The reason for this bit of precision shamed me further. When the program was designed under FDR, domestic workers — the vast majority of whom were black women — were specifically denied access to the benefits. In those days women's work was so poorly valued it was not even recognized as work. A black woman working in a white woman's kitchen was not protected by the justice of the land, only by the mercy of the woman who employed her. It took the civil rights movement (an event for which I can immediately summon a teary-eyed reverence) to overturn that terrible law.

And now I began to see the whole equation of what was devolving from my simple decision to "get help." Although Paloma wasn't paying income tax, she was still availing herself of our city's rapidly declining social services: sending her sons to public school, calling 911 when there was an emergency, driving city streets, having parties in city parks — all of which are expensive to run, none of which were benefiting from her tax dollars. And I was helping her — encouraging her — to do so.

•   •   •

THE STORY OF WHAT HAPPENED after I left that waiting room is tedious, and it involves accountants and tax forms and difficulties and considerable expense.

For a while I became the great pariah of Social Security, a fanatic with a nut cause: paying taxes. I would corner people at cocktail parties and badger them about the issue. If they admitted they weren't paying the tax, I would e-mail them links to payroll services that could take care of the paperwork for them. I wrote a convoluted and slightly insane cover story on the topic for a national magazine, after which I spent a month appearing on radio programs talking up the cause. As far as I know, I convinced exactly two people to change their ways.

Since that time I have hired a variety of women to work for me as part-time cleaners and babysitters. Each of them has completed a W-4 form the day she started, and for each I have paid not only my half of the Social Security set-aside but theirs as well. I sit them down and explain, in English and in pidgin Spanish, exactly what Social Security is, how they will become eligible, and that they should never let a senora refuse to pay it. But I know most of them will go on to take jobs without benefits.

In the end, doing the right thing has been satisfying but also not. Early in our relationship I was forever telling Paloma that she and her friends should go on strike, that if they organized and held fast, they could get more than they'd ever dreamed of — their employers depend on them, especially the working mothers who can't get out the door if the nanny doesn't show up. My own mother had supported the United Farm Workers when I was a child. She knew how to get those wicked growers to treat immigrant workers fairly: she boycotted table grapes, lettuce, Gallo wine, and whatever else was on the weekly mimeographed list that she consulted before shopping.

As a little girl I wore an orange and black button with the UFW motto — HUELGA. In my vague, liberal way I had been imagining Paloma and me aligned against The Man. What I hadn't figured out, of course, was that I was The Man. The more I legitimized our association, the more I removed it from the sphere of paternalism and sentiment and delivered it to its rightful place in the world of employment law, the more I changed the fundamental nature of the relationship.

One day, after I had made our arrangement legal — bathing myself in pride for *volunteering* to pay Social Security set-asides and workers' compensation — Paloma bounced in the front door, full of beans.

"Mrs. Kate, there's going to be a strike!"

She eagerly turned on the local news to show me what she meant. The Central American workers of Los Angeles were planning a massive two-day strike. The city would grind to a halt; the workers would force lawmakers to reconsider immigration policies.

"I'm not coming in tomorrow, okay?"

It was exactly what I had been urging her and her friends to do. But now things were different. Now, even by the most extreme definitions of the term, I wasn't exploiting her. Before I might have deserved the inconvenience of a strike. Now I didn't. Although she had every right to participate, I now had every right — moral as well as legal — to behave as an employer and not a friend.

"Okay," I said. "Don't come in." And then I said this: "But that means I won't pay you."

She looked at me in shock. I had given her more personal days than either of us could count. I had many times assessed her as too sick or too tired to work and demanded that she go home and recuperate — always with full pay.

"That's how strikes work," I said sadly.

She came in; I paid her. We were on different ground now.

●   ●   ●

AS IT TURNED OUT, my problems with motherhood were relatively short-lived. I wasn't ill suited to the vocation; I just wasn't much of a baby person. By the time the boys turned two, my mood began to lift. By the time they were three — both of them magpies, comedians, adventurers — we were off to the races. One day, about a month after their third birthday, I bought them their very first Popsicles, in the park outside a library. We sat on a blanket with our new books spread around us, one of them a nice fat novel I intended to tuck into once they finished their treats and started climbing on the jungle gym.

It was a sunny day, and Patrick's Popsicle started dripping. He stared at it in complete bewilderment, and then he said, "My ice cream is raining." At that moment I realized we had crossed into the place I had been longing for, without ever knowing it. They could talk to me. They could make sense of the world with language, and they could make me laugh with their words. I no longer felt lonely when I was alone with them. Just the opposite: they had become excellent company. That day outside the library I understood that I was happy again. We had begun.

Paloma would be with us a while longer, but each time the boys and I did something on our own — even if it was just to play in the yard together or take a picnic to the beach — the end of a relationship that had once seemed imperishable came more clearly into sight.

It was impossibly hard to break up. We would do it for trial periods — she would take a new job somewhere, but like a jealous lover with the emotional upper hand, I would woo her back. We would stand together in the kitchen while she made the terrible phone call, and then we'd sag against the counters in relief. But eventually it had to end.

After Paloma left for good, the boys missed her violently for a while, and she missed them, too. Sometimes, she would call from her new job to hear their voices. Just last weekend she stopped by to cook soup for them. They were at a birthday party, so I leaned against the kitchen door and entertained her with stories about them while she stood at my counter, chopping the potatoes and carrots she had brought with her. I was hoping they would be back in time to see her, but the party ran late, and she left the pot of soup on the back burner, with a lid to keep it warm.

Executive Child

SOMETIMES WHEN I SIT at my desk orchestrating my children's lives — efficiently completing hot lunch order forms and day camp applications, ordering team T-shirts and birthday party presents by the dozen — I feel more like an executive assistant than a mother. My children lead lives like those of corporate vice presidents, their days planned months in advance. I have Miss Moneypenny's romantic attachment to my little bosses, as well as her sterling loyalty and eagerness to stand in the shadows, taking pleasure in the achievements — impossible without her steadying, invisible hand — of the loved ones.

In short I am a modern mother, one whose love for her children is manifested not only in a primal concern for their safety and nurture but also in the selection of activities and classes that shape the hours of their childhoods. Striking the perfect balance between structured and unstructured time is one of our central preoccupations. Introduce the phrase "overscheduled child" as a conversational gambit in my circle, and you'll get an earful: it's a damnable practice, a pox on family life, an oppressive force weighing down on all that is most cherished and magical about childhood. Yet midway through this heated oration, there is always a moment when the speaker realizes that this derision is hitting uncomfortably close to home. In tones at once defensive and adamant, a declaration is made: "Of course, *my* kids aren't overscheduled." Just as the definition of a nymphomaniac is a person who has more sex than you, an overscheduled child is one enrolled in more classes than yours. We may cavil about the burden that all of this places on family life, but none of us is prepared to stand down: come T-ball sign-ups or tennis camp registration, we're all there, checkbooks in hand.

Theories about the evolution and meaning of this kind of parenting are legion, but in my case the enrollment of my small children in a roster of activities had nothing to do with their academic prospects or intellectual development. It had only to do with the fact that after they were born, I began losing my mind.

•   •   •

I REMEMBER THE FIRST YEAR and a half of my children's lives as being marked by a combination of elation and the low-level depression that dogs shut-ins the world over. My husband had taken a big corporate job to pay for the type of motherhood I had chosen to pursue, which involved round-the-clock worry about the babies and extremely infrequent separations from them. He was gone from seven in the morning until seven or eight at night, and I was lonely.

The babies and I were invited many places — to a gathering of mothers in the park, to a meeting of a twins-only playgroup at a friend's house — and I would mark these events on my calendar, sincerely intending to go to them. But when the appointed hour arrived, something always went wrong. One of the babies would suddenly demand an unscheduled feeding, or they would both suddenly knock off into a deep sleep, which only a fool would fail to recognize as a sign from God himself that it was time to make a cup of tea and chat on the telephone. It was my friends from work whom I longed for — full of gossip and talk of important matters — not the mothers in the park, who were either just as depressed as I was or spilling over with talk of diapers and breast milk and colic, topics with which I was similarly obsessed but which cheered me not at all to discuss ad infinitum.

Slowly the invitations dried up, and I became one of those out-of-sync, somewhat pitiable mothers, patrolling the streets with my enormous stroller during odd hours, spending far too much time in front of the television in my zip-front chenille bathrobe, getting in trouble at Starbucks for letting the babies pull bags of coffee off the rack while I was reading. My sister called from London and tactfully suggested I get a weekend babysitter and go out with my husband a little more often. My mother thought I should go back to work. People were starting to get a little worried about me.

And then one day I managed to get the three of us to the Westside Pavilion shopping mall for a desperately needed change of pace. We were performing a tour of inspection of the top floor, when I caught sight of several mothers purposefully pushing their strollers through the double doors of an establishment I'd never noticed before. I rolled my own stroller over and took a curious look at the yellow letters painted on the plate glass window: TUMBLE CAMP. It turned out to be a children's gym, with classes starting for babies as young as six months. I'd heard of such places, but I had thought they were for older children. Inside I was given a roster of classes, informed that tuition was nonrefundable, and shown the elaborate security procedures, whereby individual name tags would be printed by the computer every time we took a class. I joined immediately.

If motherhood abruptly wrested me from the world of adult enterprise, Tumble Camp put me back in business. It restored to me many of the things I had missed from work: an inflexible schedule, a sense of purpose, and colleagues engaged in a common pursuit. The classes were blessedly short and as focused as a board meeting: we sang a song, the mothers jollied the children through an obstacle course that changed every week, there was some free time, and then there was a good-bye song and hand stamps for the kids. The program was supposed to inculcate skills in the children — balance and coordination, and so on — but I knew that was a bunch of hooey. Every normally developing kid gains those skills naturally if he spends enough time in a playground or a backyard. But I wasn't there to improve the children; they were already perfect as far as I was concerned. What I liked was that I had a series of climate-controlled, time-limited, intensive little seminars to go to and a way of imposing structure on the endless, ungraspable days of early parenthood.

In due time I discovered that Tumble Camp was not the only game in town. There were also classes at outfits called Fit for Kids and Bright Child, and I enrolled in them, too. Our church nursery school offered a parent-toddler program once a week, which turned out to be a kind of pre-preschool, its core philosophy reminding me of the old Texas expression, "I'm fixin' to get ready to start." The zoo had classes for toddlers, as did the Natural History Museum and the YMCA. Before long we had something to do every day of the week; sometimes we had to eat lunch at McDonald's or the mall food court because we had two engagements. The boys, I'm sure, would have been just as happy with a daily trip to the park, but they took to the new routine willingly enough, and some of the classes we loved. We took Music and Motion from a beautiful young woman known to us as Miss Simona, and we all became quite taken with her. Patrick would murmur her name when he was falling asleep, and I would think of her brown eyes and complicated personal life (her husband had recently left her) whenever I played one of the two sing-along cassettes she had sold to us for forty dollars.

My life began to improve. The babies learned the one thing none of the classes taught — how to talk — and with that my loneliness began to abate. One day when I was loading the backpack for class, I sneezed, and from somewhere down near the floor a tiny voice said, "Bless you." In that moment I realized that what my shrink had been telling me every week was in fact true: the babies would get older; things would get easier. On a sunny October day the boys started nursery school five mornings a week. When I walked through my front door after dropping them off, my footsteps echoed on the hardwood floors of the empty house, and I realized that a chapter of my life had come to an end. I gave away the chenille robe and took the safety rails off the boys' beds. A few months

148

later, when I was tidying up, I found one of Miss Simona's cassettes in a kitchen drawer, and I threw it in the trash. We had emerged.

•   •   •

THE ACTIVITIES, however, stayed with us. The boys are first graders now, and they are a blur of motion. On Mondays Patrick takes an after-school class called Mad Science, on Tuesdays Conor plays T-Ball, and on Saturdays they both have basketball and an hour of semiprivate soccer coaching. Their school has an extended-day program — two hours of supervised play, art projects, and a snack — of which they are both exceedingly fond. They are yellow belts in karate; they take the occasional tennis lesson; they swim. In addition to these various lessons and classes, they have an intense and carefully structured playdate schedule, as well as a ceaseless round of birthday parties to attend. There is Sunday school, of course, and at school they are also quite busy, making action paintings in the style of Jackson Pollock, testing the pH balance of various liquids, working on computers, being introduced to and horrified by slavery, copying the complex patterns of Navajo blankets.

The boys are bullish on this schedule, but it is both a

boon and a burden to me. I'm delighted to watch my sons happily engaged in one fun project or another, growing ever more accomplished at things I have never attempted, palling around with their numberless friends. These classes, of course, are expensive, and it is a point of pride to me that I am able to provide them to my children, just as (so long ago) it was a point of pride to my mother that she was able to provide her children with trips to Disneyland and a shining mountain of new toys every Christmas. Each generation hopes for more. But there is also a relentless, exhausting nature to this whirl of events, a sense that the children — barely seven years old — are engaged in the most important work of the household, that I must be ever vigilant about our schedule to ensure that we don't miss a lesson or a team photo or a trophy ceremony. In the long run, the extra hours that this program buys me are dwarfed by the amount of time and energy it takes to keep the thing up and running; it's a beast that must be thrown fresh meat daily. The roster of after-school activities offered at my sons' school includes not just Roving Reporters, Animal Invasion, and Lullaby of Broadway, but also a class called Meditation and Yoga for Parents and Teachers. The image this conjures — of scores of tots furiously reporting the news and belting out "Second Hand Rose," while somewhere in their midst a cloistered cell of harassed adults tries desperately to unwind from it all — is mildly comical. Still, if I could find the time, I would take the class.

The old-fashioned, wholesome activities of the fifties and sixties — scouting, for example — have become less popular because yuppie parents, obsessed with status and flush with the cash of the new professional class, believe that enterprises like the Boy Scouts suggest the exact kind of middle-middle-class earnestness that they eschew most powerfully. They are attracted to the pastimes of the American aristocracy, as they imagine it: tennis and soccer, art and advanced academics. What nobody seemed prepared for is the extent to which these activities would come to dominate family life.

●　　　●　　　●

MANAGING THE NEW BUSYNESS has become a major concern for millions of American families, and there are shelves full of books devoted to helping meet the challenge. One set of books maintains that families should conduct themselves like efficient little businesses, with parents thinking of their children's various lessons and sports commitments as so many board meetings: non-negotiable, crucially important, and best approached with a maximum of preparation. According to this line of thinking, the children are mini-executives, and the parents function as their assistants, syncing up schedules, filling out reams of applications, and keeping medical forms and tuition payments up to date.

The most famous of the family-as-corporation books is Stephen Covey's *7 Habits of Highly Effective Families*, the successful offspring of his 1989 phenomenon, *The 7 Habits of Highly Effective People*, one of the best-selling books of all time. If Covey had a moment's pause about appropriating the language and strategies of the business world and applying them to family life, it doesn't show up in the text. "You want to prioritize your family," he tells us at the outset, a goal best achieved by getting clear on your vision and bringing the team together to write a mission statement, an opportunity to "get everyone's ideas and feelings out on the table." The family should have weekly meetings, with the mission statement posted nearby for easy reference. The gathering should be charged with purpose — the kids providing executive summaries of their trials and achievements, the parents responding with a download of the family's values and beliefs. Readers are encouraged to make the most of this time. They might keep a set of the *World Book Encyclopedia* to hand so that if one of the little shavers wonders aloud about, say, Rhode Island — "Gee, Dad, how small *is* it?" — reliable, accurate information can be immediately disseminated.

Like many books on this subject, Covey's proceeds

from the notion that raising children is complicated, that it cannot be approached in the same muddle-through-and-hope-for-the-best method by which the children were initially created. To be an effective parent, one must master not only the seven habits ("Be Proactive"; "Synergize"), but also understand the five unique human gifts, the four primary laws of love, the two time-organizing structures, and the eleven essential principles. Like many self-help books, Covey's is larded with inspirational quotations (which suggest less a lifetime's careful reading of the great books than an afternoon's purposeful paging through *Bartlett's Familiar Quotations*) and with testimonials from people who have applied his principles to raising their children. To read their stories is to get the sense of a generation of Americans as puzzled by their own families as Margaret Mead once was by the Samoans. One family, after creating their mission statement, took a vacation wearing matching T-shirts, which caused a gas station attendant to remark that they looked like a team. Says the proud father, "That just kind of cemented it. We looked at one another and felt an incredible high. We got back in the car and took off, windows down, radio cranked up, ice cream melting in the backseat. We were a family!"

The key to the system is time management. Covey, who travels extensively for work, experienced his parenting low point when he found himself in a Chicago hotel room on the night of his daughter's appearance in a high school production of *West Side Story:* "The feeling in my heart was one of deep regret. . . . Somehow Colleen's play had gotten lost in the press of work and other demands, and I simply didn't have it on my calendar." The bottom line: "If you really want to prioritize your family, you simply have to plan ahead and be strong." This is appointment parenting, in which simply being around for the kids day in and day out is not important. What matters most is making it to their high-priority games and performances. Scheduling is everything. Covey is part owner of a hugely successful consulting firm, which offers not only "solutions for business" and an online mission statement builder, but also an "Elementary School Planner" that is "geared to ages 6–12 and encourages students to start each week by setting personal learning and caring goals and to reflect on these at the end of the week." Unmentioned is the fact that this practice clearly feeds the beast of over-scheduling: when kids and teachers get the message that parents care only about performances and big games, these events — and the preparation they require — tend to loom ever larger on the horizon.

Like most contemporary writers on family life, Covey is mesmerized by the practice of sitting down to dinner, a custom he imbues with almost magical properties to bind and focus a family. It is also an excellent opportunity for multitasking. Everyone should report for grub with both their calendars and their hearts open. You never know when Sissy's going to announce a swim meet or Dad's going to impart a gem of platitudinous counsel. The business model holds that all of the salubrious effects of family dinner can be crammed into a once-a-week event, thereby freeing busy parents from the need to make it to the table every night. What Covey fails to consider is that with everybody scheduled to the teeth, that weekly slice of time is going to look mighty attractive. *Organizing from the Inside Out for Teens* is a book written by master organizer Julie Morgenstern and her daughter Jessi (sixteen years old and "a student, dancer, activist, journalist, and writer"). In it teens are tendered the following helpful hint: "Ask your parents if you can skip family dinner once a week, eating a light meal on your own to make time for rehearsal." Given that so many parents grace the dinner table only once a week, the suggestion has a certain rich irony that brought back to me the deeply felt sense of poetic justice I once experienced listening to the lyrics of "Cat's in the Cradle."

     •   •   •

THE POLAR OPPOSITE approach to these conditions is taken by a gathering social movement that calls for a radical restructuring of family life, a romantic return to the simpler routines of an earlier time. In the bestseller *The*

Shelter of Each Other, psychologist Mary Pipher describes in glowing terms the lives of her midwestern grandparents, who didn't let the hardships of farming an unforgiving piece of land in the thirties keep them from showering each other with affection and support. Pipher concludes that their lives were in fact more rewarding and satisfying than those of the financially comfortable yet hopelessly harried two-career families she sees in her practice. The book's premise is simple and appealing: troubled families, she suggests, can be healed without complicated mission statements or weekly meetings; they need only watch a few episodes of *The Waltons* and try to revive some of the jolliness and homemade fun for which the Great Depression is justly famous.

Several communities have lately made a splash by inaugurating programs devoted to similar goals. Ridgewood, New Jersey's Ready, Set, *Relax!* urges families to set aside one night each year on which they forgo extracurricular activities, turn off the television set, and spend time together, all the while reflecting on whether they are happy with the way they usually spend their evenings. Wayzata, Minnesota's Putting Family First is an even more successful organization. Its philosophy and methods are outlined in a book called *Putting Family First,* by William J. Doherty and Barbara Z. Carlson, who urge families to "get off the merry-go-round" and reclaim the quiet sanctity of the domestic lives of a bygone era. Once again it's family dinner to the rescue: we learn that research clearly links it with "a wide range of positive outcomes." Refreshingly the authors don't let parents off the hook with a once-a-week appearance. However, like Covey, they are loath to poach hours from adults' all-consuming careers. The meal, they suggest, may be served as late as ten o'clock at night, or indeed anytime before midnight, a proposal that might be practical if one is raising a family of thirty-five-year-old nightclub performers.

This preposterous suggestion is just one of a raft of curious recommendations proffered in a chapter on family meals that suggests that one of the most enduring human activities, the communal eating of food, has become as puzzling and foreign a habit as to have been freshly cribbed from the animal kingdom. Readers are advised to inaugurate their return to family dinner not by setting the table and preheating the oven, but by filling out a complicated chart called "Who's Here?" to reveal who's been tying on the feedbag and who's been AWOL. A section titled "Creating Family Dinner Rituals" includes queries — "How are family members called to the table? Is there a struggle?" — that hint at how bad things may be in Dinnerland, USA. ("Chow's on. Somebody hog-tie Sammy.") Once the assessment has been concluded and analyzed, dinner can be prepared and eventually even served — but only after calling everyone to table via a "special method" such as ringing a gong, playing a song on the piano, or singing a designated ditty. Mom and Dad need to monitor dinner conversation closely: it should be evenly divided between "logistics talk" and "connection talk." Toward that end we are provided lists of child-friendly conversation starters ("Would you rather be a Porsche or a Jeep?"). And if things get ho-hum, the author suggests some exotic dining locations (under the table, on a picnic blanket in front of the fire) that sound more like advice for juicing up a wilting sex life than getting some macaroni and cheese into the kids.

Clearly all of these writers share a certain confusion about dinner's role in family life: can it be a once-a-week ritualized gathering, or should it be an ongoing kiddie carnival, served in the dead of night, underneath the table? One thing, however, is clear: their notions about the meal and its importance in family life are rooted in middle-class American assumptions about how and when parents and children ought to interact. What they are loath to admit is that the great missing element of that kind of existence is not dinner gongs or lists of conversation starters. It's a kind of family life in which expectations have not been raised, but radically lowered.

It requires a mother who considers putting dinner on the table neither an exalted nor a menial task, and also a collection of family members whose worldly ambitions are low enough that they all happen to be hanging around the house at six-thirty. For family life to mimic the postwar ideal that is our current fixation, we would need to revive the cultural traditions that created it: the one-income family, the middle-class tendency toward frugality, and the understanding that one's children's prospects won't include elite private colleges and stratospheric professional success, both of which may hinge on tremendous achievements in the world of extracurricular activities.

If children are to have unstructured time, they need a mother at home; no one would advocate a new generation of latchkey children. But she must be a certain kind of mother — one willing to divest her sense of purpose from her children's achievement. She must be a woman willing to forgo the prestige of professional life in order to sit home while her kids dream up new games out in the tree house and wait for her to call them in for a nourishing dinner. She must be willing to endure the humiliation of forgoing a career and of raising tots bound for state college.

•　　•　　•

NOT LONG AGO, my son Conor's kindergarten T-ball team played their big game with halftime entertainment provided by the cheerleading club (grades K–3). Societal Cassandras would have been deeply disappointed by the event, which was sweetness itself. There wasn't a joyless child in the house, and nary an absentee parent either. The cheerleaders were short on military precision and long on exuberance; the game was of the no-outs, no-score variety. Play was briefly interrupted when an outfielder wandered over to his mother and tried to climb in her lap. He was gently encouraged to return to his post, where he dreamily scuffed the gym floor with his sneaker and waited out the inning. There were doughnuts and trophies for all.

Still, a lot was riding on the game. The husband next to me whispered to his wife that he had canceled two meetings to get there, and she immediately averred that she'd canceled one herself. My husband arrived late, having left the office in the midst of a minor crisis; he would resume a conference call in his car after the game. The working mothers arrived exactly on time, a precision team. They click-clacked to their seats and fished tiny video cameras out of enormous purses. It was as though a significant swath of the professional and financial life of Los Angeles had been temporarily frozen in midaction — meetings abandoned, e-mail messages piling up, cell phones set to vibrate — so that a group of highly paid senior executives could watch some five-year-olds play ball. Impervious to these tensions were the at-home mothers who had arrived early and reserved blocks of seats, and who were chatting expansively with one another. Many of them had toddlers in tow, and they passed down snacks and sippy cups of juice as they talked. Why shouldn't they make a day of it? Having time to be fully present for their children is exactly why most of them don't work.

That working and nonworking mothers are pitting themselves against one another in a battle to the death has become a media cliché. Still, as with many so cultural phenomena, the intensity of after-school activities has everything to do with the different needs of these two factions. When I was a full-time mother, I needed Tumble Camp to help fill my days in a certain way — one that imitated the routines and rhythms of work. And now that I am a writer, my days are filled with actual work. If my boys take a class after school, I gain an extra hour to work.

Working and nonworking mothers are building a culture together, however unwittingly. It is a culture that responds to the emotional needs of these mothers as much as — if not more than — to the developmental needs of their children. When I went to Tumble Camp to keep myself entertained, the working mothers of my acquaintance worried that their own infants might get shortchanged by not getting ridiculously early exposure to circle time and balance beams. So they started trying to get out of work one morning a week to take their own babies to the class. When I'm supposed to be writing but hear that the at-home mothers are showing up in force for soccer practice — an event that was supposed to buy me an extra hour of time — I'm in the minivan and headed to the park in a nanosecond. I'm not going to have my children be the ones whose mother doesn't show up for them. And so it goes.

Activities are what prevent us from having two classes of kids within the same social class. All of the children are doing the same things; it's the mothers, these days, who bear the brunt of the new culture they are creating, caviling about the intensity of modern motherhood even as they ratchet up that intensity with each passing month.

When the T-ball players emerged through a side door, the parents went wild. There were hoots and cheers, and dozens of cameras flashed and whirred. When I caught sight of Conor (lollygagging at the end of the line and making silly faces at the crowd), I was so overcome with tenderness that for an embarrassing moment I thought I might cry. It was a kind of mass hysteria, entirely benign and fueled by nothing but love, but any observer would surely have noticed the extent to which such games and performances are entwined with how we see ourselves as parents. Public events are central to what we tell ourselves and one another about how much we love our children: *Look, I'm here! I stopped everything just to come.*

After the T-ball game my husband took a final roll of pictures and congratulated the coaches, then he headed off to his conference call. Conor and I walked outside in the hot sunshine, triumphant with our new trophy. There is a climbing structure outside the gym, and he scrambled up it as quickly as a cat. I gazed up at him. He is a cosseted, late-life child, and we have given him the best of everything: Playmobil villages and expensive education, T-ball and tennis and swimming. He will have more than we had. When his class needs a chaperone for a field trip — or eight bottles of lemon-flavored Perrier for the teachers' lunch, or three dozen nut-free brownies for the kindergarten picnic, or someone to pass out the hot lunches or collect the used clothes and shoes for Operation School Bell — I stop whatever I'm doing and go there. I would sooner miss a blood transfusion than an open house.

Conor was happy up there on top of the jungle gym — happier, in fact, than he'd been in the outfield (he was the child who wandered off). But I quickly lost interest in standing around the hot playground, especially when we had so many other things to do. "Okay," I said brightly, "come down." It was a busy afternoon; we needed to get going.

Drudges and Celebrities: The New Housekeeping

IF IT HAD BEEN SUGGESTED to my mother, who ran a pretty tight ship, that she spend thirty minutes watching a television show in which a college-educated millionaire instructed her on the proper way to sweep a floor, she would have laughed. She knew how to sweep a floor, she did it efficiently, and then she was on to the next thing. I, on the other hand, have a devil of a time sweeping all the bits into the dustpan, and I confess to a sudden bout of sullenness — and a distinct feeling of oppression — whenever I attempt such a thing. Unlike my mother, however, sweeping the floor is an act I spend considerable time thinking about, if not doing. And this is why I am a follower of Martha Stewart, while she was not.

To understand our very different attitudes toward housekeeping, you have to understand the attitudes of the women who came between us, many of whom thought that the simple tasks such as making beds and washing dishes could potentially ensnare them in a millennia-old trap of patriarchy and dashed ambition. I remember being sent in 1977, at age fifteen, to my very first psychothera-pist, a young wife and mother with a capacious office on Bancroft Avenue. I can't remember a thing I talked about on all those darkening afternoons, but I do remember very clearly a day on which she suddenly sat up straight in her chair and began discussing, for reasons I could not fathom and in the most heated terms imaginable, not the vagaries of my sullen adolescence, but, rather, marriage — specifically, her own. "I mean, who's going to do the shit work?" she asked angrily. "Who's going to make the pancakes?"

I stared at her uncomprehendingly. The only wife I knew intimately was my mother, who certainly had her discontents, but whom I couldn't even imagine using the term "shit work," let alone using it to characterize the making of pancakes — something she did regularly, compe-tently, and, as far as I could tell, happily. (She liked pancakes; so did the rest of us.) But in 1978 shit work was becoming a real problem. Shit work, in fact, was threatening to put the brakes on the women's movement. Joan Didion's un-paralleled 1972 essay on the movement ("To make an omelette," the essay begins, "you need not only those broken eggs but someone 'oppressed' to break them") describes the attempts women of the era made to arrive at an equitable division of household labor:

They totted up the pans scoured, the towels picked off the bathroom floor, the loads of laundry done in a lifetime. Cooking a meal could only be "dog-work," and to claim any pleasure from it was evidence of craven acquiescence in one's own forced labor. Small children could only be odious mechanisms for the spilling and digesting of food, for robbing women of their "freedom." It was a long way from Simone de Beauvoir's grave and awesome recognition of woman's role as "the Other" to the notion that the first step in changing that role was Alix Kates Shulman's marriage contract ("wife strips beds, husband remakes them").

Alix Kates Shulman's marriage contract, which I have read, is so perfectly a document of its time that it might stand alone, a kind of synecdoche for twenty years' worth of arguing and slamming doors and fuming over the notorious inability of husbands to fold a fitted sheet or get the children's breakfast on the table without leaving behind a scrim of crumbs and jelly on every flat surface in the room. Originally published in 1970, in a feminist magazine called *Up from Under,* the contract — like the women's liberation movement itself — quickly moved from the radical margins of society to its very center. It was reprinted in the debut issue of *Ms.,* no surprise, but also in *Redbook, New York,* and *Life,* in which it was part of a cover story on the subject of experimental marriages. (That a marriage in which the husband helped out with the housework qualified as "experimental" tells you how much things have changed in the past three decades.) It was also taken seriously in some very high quarters, including the standard Harvard textbook on contract law, in which it was reprinted.

The document, which I first encountered when I read the Didion essay as a girl, struck me as odd. I could see how a bride on the eve of her wedding could think ahead to the making and unmaking of beds (although it was only once I was deep into marriage that it occurred to me this task might be a chore, as opposed to yet another delightful aspect of married sexuality, which I could imagine only in the most thrilling terms), but there was other language in it that seemed born of actual and bitter experience. Shulman and her husband, for example, were going to divide "the week into hours during which the children were to address their 'personal questions' to either one parent or another." It was difficult for me to conceive of a bride's coming up with such a disillusioned view of the thing, even a bride fully alerted to the oppression of motherhood. But it turns out that Shulman was no bride when she wrote it. I have since learned that her marriage agreement — talk about a doomed cause — was of the postnuptial variety.

Alix Kates Shulman's marriage — under way a full decade before she sat down at her typewriter, aglow with "feminist irony, idealism, audacity, and glee," and punched out the notorious contract — had been buffeted by many of the forces at play in American cultural life of the late sixties and early seventies, but she and her husband evinced an impressive ability to up the ante. He worked; she stayed home with the kids and wrote "subversive" essays, short stories, and position papers, all of which centered on her growing desire to come Up From Under. He retaliated by starting a new business venture in another state and taking up with a UC Berkeley student. She double-retaliated by taking a young lover of her own and publishing an essay about her husband's inability to bring her to orgasm, an essay that ended with the half-jaunty, half-exasperated imperative "Think clitoris!" At this point Alix and her husband were apparently seized by the one patently sensible idea of their entire marriage: they needed to get divorced.

Now the story begins to get complicated. In the early seventies there was no such thing as joint custody in the state of New York, and Alix realized that a divorce was not going to be much of a boon to her, since it would leave her with the kids full-time, which would mean a heck of a lot of breakfasts to prepare and lunch boxes to pack — activities that would sorely cut into the time available for her to make pronouncements on behalf of the voiceless clitoris. When friends heard about her rotten marriage and asked her when she was going to divorce the bum, she would snappily reply, "Not until you're ready to help me take care of my kids." Thus the marriage agreement — which Shulman originally, and more accurately, wanted to title "A Divorce Dilemma and a Marriage Agreement" — was born, a way to husk the marriage of any pretense of emotional fulfillment and reduce it to a purely labor-sharing arrangement. (Her husband signed it, ran off with his coed, and then — proving himself to be one of the great masochists of the twentieth century — returned to Shulman for another full decade of punishment before they finally switched off the lights.)

The marriage agreement virtually demanded to be ridiculed, and ridiculed it was: not only by Joan Didion but also by Russell Baker and Norman Mailer. (In his 1971 antifeminist manifesto *The Prisoner of Sex,* Mailer considered the agreement at some length, concluding that he "would not be married to such a woman." The potential of the agreement to serve as a lifetime protection policy against marriage to Norman Mailer makes me half want to hold on to my own copy, just to be on the safe side.) Certainly Shulman has earned herself a spot on almost any short list of very silly people. Yet I am reluctant to make too much sport of her document, or of the countless similar ones it inspired. I am a wife and mother of young children in a very different time from Shulman's, a time that is in many respects more brutal and more brutalizing, a time that has been morally coarsening for many of us, a time that has made hypocrites of many contemporary feminists in ways that Shulman and her sisters in arms were not hypocrites. I have never once argued with my husband about which of us was going to change the sheets of the marriage bed, but then, to my certain knowledge, neither one of us ever has changed the sheets. Or scrubbed the bathtubs, or dusted the cobwebs off the top of the living room bookcase, or used the special mop and the special noncorrosive cleanser on the hardwood floors. The maid has. Two years ago our little boys got stomach flu, one right after the other, and there were ever so many loads of wash to do, but we did not do them. The nanny did.

You have to give those old libbers their due: they spent a lot of time thinking about the unpleasantness of housework and the unfairness of its age-old tendency to fall upon women. They were loath, they claimed, to foist such demeaning work on other human beings. (Well, not all of them were loath. Betty Friedan had a crack cleaning woman on staff when she was busy writing about the oppression of domestic work.) Indeed Shulman's contract specifies that the "burden" of the cleaning work should not be placed on "someone hired from outside." Members of the women's movement believed that it was of great importance, politically and psychologically, for men to share equally in the care of households and children. Further, feminists of the period had also thought deeply about race, and about the tendency of white women to shape comfortable lives around the toil and suffering of black women.

The members of a thousand consciousness-raising groups drove themselves into a thousand tizzies trying to think up a solution to this homely yet vexing problem. The notorious Wages for Housework campaign ("WE WANT IT IN CASH, RETROACTIVE AND IMMEDIATELY. AND WE WANT ALL OF IT") came to naught. Pat Mainardi's much-read *The Politics of Housework* included many strategies for cajoling a reluctant male into taking on some washing and cooking, from the deeply Marxist ("Arm yourself with some knowledge of the psychology of oppressed peoples") to the stubbornly practical ("Use timesheets"). But you can know chapter and verse about the psychology of oppressed peoples and still not get a man to turn out a nice meal — the rice ready at the same time as the meat — come the end of a long day. Communes, which had offered the promise of a collective approach to domestic work, turned out to be yet another bust. As Vivian Estellachild wrote in 1971, the typical hippie commune's recruitment ad could have read, "Wanted: groovy, well-built chick to share apartment and do the cooking and cleaning."

Certainly there was a bit of hope in the abandonment of bourgeois housekeeping standards, something that the most radical factions were demanding and that even the less political groups saw as promising. *The Feminine Mystique* has its roots in a questionnaire that Betty Friedan sent to her Smith College classmates on the occasion of their fifteenth reunion. Included on it were questions one might expect: "Did you have career ambitions?" "Who manages the family finances, you or your husband?" But there were also these two telling questions: "Do you put the milk bottle on the table? Use paper napkins?" Milk decanted into a pitcher and a linen napkin beside the breakfast plate — the physical embodiment of an approach to daily life that included moments of grace and loveliness, that showed (to use the old phrase) a woman's touch — suddenly seemed the very stuff of oppression. But even with the fillips abandoned, with the milk plunked down on the table and the kids wiping at grotty faces with paper napkins, there was still a heck of a lot of housework and child care that simply couldn't be streamlined.

In one of history's great moments, Betty Friedan once took her road show to Columbus, Ohio, where Erma Bombeck and her friends were busy keeping house and raising children. "None of us had ever heard of Betty Friedan," Bombeck later wrote, "but we would have watched a slide show of the History of Paper Clips to get out of the daily drudge detail. We all climbed in Charmaine's station wagon with the wood on it and set off to be entertained." They were not entertained; they were harangued. "The small, stocky, mussed woman took the stage, and we were cheered. She looked like one of us." Friedan went on a rant about screaming children and dirty laundry, and Bombeck and her friends laughed encouragingly; these were the comic elements of their lives. Friedan, however, was not amused. She began screaming at her confused audience: none of this was funny; this was a tragedy. She told the women that they were living lives of quiet desperation; the suburbs were a concentration camp. She told them they didn't need men and that they shouldn't live through their children and husbands.

The audience was stunned and silent. "There was some truth to what she was saying," recalled Bombeck, but on the whole Friedan was "counting on an anger among midwestern women that didn't yet exist." Like Friedan, Bombeck found housewifery tedious. Unlike Friedan, she hadn't lost sight of its higher purpose: "I had a life going here. Maybe it needed work, but I had a husband and three kids whom I loved and I wasn't ready to discard anything."

I remember, during that time, knowing many girls whose mothers gave up. There would be squalor beyond reckoning in the kitchen, and sometimes the basic functions of the rooms had been corrupted. There was a house in which the dining room had been converted into a flop-house. I knew a girl whose parents were at war, leaving the daughter and mother alone in a big Craftsman house without a stick of furniture save a console television in the living room. Women were getting into ceramics and militant poetry writing. Talent was a prerequisite for neither occupation; all that was needed was a smoldering anger. Putting on lipstick was an oppressive act. Cooking nourishing dinners was an oppressive act. The mothers in those houses were sullen or absent, or they were wrapped in batik and committed to the cooking of ethnic dishes. They would have hideous caches of broken eggshells and wet coffee grounds squirreled away on kitchen counters, waiting to be delivered to the compost heaps. One girl I knew came to school with matted hair every day because her mother had given up brushing it — too oppressive.

There was nothing to admire about these women, nothing about their lives that inspired dreaminess. They were half-liberated, half-imprisoned, angry all the time.

Everything those women dreamed of — equal opportunity in the workplace, maternity leave, and laws against sexual harassment — came to pass in a surprisingly short period of time. That the world has changed is due, in some measure, to the women who wore batik and stopped ironing their husband's shirts. All the while, there was a Connecticut housewife who was preparing to build an empire on the notion that ironing and polishing silver and sweeping a kitchen floor might offer an almost sacred communion with what is most essentially and attractively feminine. What they could not have predicted was that housekeeping, or at least a glamorized approximation of the art, was about to make a raging comeback in the person of its new champion: Martha Stewart.

Biographers and journalists have spent a quarter century trying to make sense of Stewart's appeal to women like me, and they invariably tend to dismiss the very heart of her success: the incontrovertible fact of her tremendous style. The photography in her various publications seems to reduce all of female longing to its essential elements. A basket of flowers, a child's lawn pinafore draped across a painted rocking chair, an exceptionally white towel folded in thirds and perched in glamorous isolation on a clean and barren shelf. Most of the pictures feature a lot of sunlight, and many show rooms that are either empty of people or occupied solely by Martha, evoking the profound and enduring female desires for solitude and silence. No heterosexual man can understand this stuff, and no woman with a beating heart and an ounce of femininity can resist it. I can unpack a paragraph of Martha Stewart prose with the best of them, but I also fall mute and wondering at the pages of *Martha Stewart Living*.

Stewart's aesthetic has been steadily evolving over the past two decades, untrammeled by either criticism or prison time. At this point it has reached a peak of almost unbearable perfection. To compare her two wedding volumes, published in 1987 and 1999, is to see just how far things have come. The first appeared at the precise moment when Americans by the millions were returning to formal weddings. In fact its publication was so timely and so influential that it's hard to know to what extent Stewart predicted the craze and to what extent she created it. The book has a documentary quality. It features photographs of actual weddings she catered during the summers of 1984 and 1985 and also some that she heard about and asked if she might photograph and include in the book. The pictures are full of the mess and indignity of real life. There are a few unattractive brides and a couple of chubby ones (as well as several couples of such heartrending youth and hopefulness that I banished a vague notion of doing a longitudinal study of the fate of these marriages as soon as it flitted through my head). There are wedding guests in shorts and shirtsleeves, several preparing to board a Greyhound bus, a couple of Porta Potties nestled into a leafy corner of a reception site. On one table there's a two-liter bottle of Coca-Cola, on another a fifth of cheap Scotch.

To look at the more recent volume is to see all this unpleasantness burnished away. Actual brides are for the most part relegated to small black-and-white photographs. The full-color spreads feature models and careful art direction and receptions unsullied by actual guests.

The venues for these stage-set weddings seem to be a collection of New England chapels of the highest caliber. Whitewashed shingles and gleaming wooden pews provide austere backdrops for garlands of flowers, wreaths of flowers, paper cones of flowers. Espaliered bushes are covered in clouds of white tulle and tied with silk ribbons. Walkways are blanketed with thick drifts of petals. Oak trees are hung with white Japanese lanterns. Flower girls wear wreaths of roses and carry more of them. Winter weddings feature severe Christmas trees and tall centerpieces of sugared fruit.

My attraction to these images is rooted in a simple truth: women like pretty things. Stewart's magazines (she has four titles: *Living, Baby, Kids,* and *Weddings*) all seem to depict some parallel universe in which loveliness and order are untrammeled by the surging chaos of life in session, particularly life as it is lived with small children. In an issue of *Martha Stewart Kids,* I saw a photograph of a pair of old-fashioned white baby shoes with their laces replaced by two lengths of grosgrain ribbon. The result was impractical in the extreme — and very, very pretty. Which is a fair summation of many Stewart projects. In one of the few apt observations in Christopher Byron's best-selling and nasty biography *Martha Inc.,* he calls Stewart's "the face of the age." I would also say that the look of her magazines has become the look of women's magazines of the age. The photography, art direction, and layouts in many contemporary publications — including the magazine *Real Simple,* the redesigned *Child,* and all the craft and decorating features in the mainstream women's magazines — are clearly and deeply influenced by Stewart's.

Much of the Stewart enterprise, of course, involves a certain level of fantasy and wish fulfillment, having to do not only with the old dreams of wealth and elegance but also with the new one of time. That many of Stewart's projects are time-consuming is in fact part of their appeal. A risibly complicated recipe for sandwiches that are a "tempting snack for a 1-year-old," which ran in a recent issue of *Baby* (flower-shaped, their bright yellow centers were created by mashing cooked egg yolk with butter, rolling the resulting paste into a tube, wrapping the tube in parchment paper, refrigerating it, and then slicing it into half-inch-thick rounds), is attractive not in spite of its ludicrous complexity, but because of it. *Imagine having enough time to do something like that!*

The question of whether Stewart is indeed the "teacher" she has always professed to be or whether she is a kind of performance artist is an old one. I think that a significant number of women, including some of Stewart's staunchest defenders, appreciate what she does but never personally attempt it. *Martha Stewart Living* is filled with recipes for complicated restaurant-type food — caramelized fennel, warm goat cheese with wasabi-pea crust, and the like — but the ads are for Wendy's Mandarin

Chicken Salad, Hormel's precooked roast beef, and Jell-O. One gets the sense that women enjoy reading about the best way to select a leg of lamb, but when it's dinnertime they give an exhausted shrug and settle for the ease and convenience of Campbell's 2-Step Beefy Taco Joes, the recipe for which appears in a Campbell's ad in the magazine's hundredth issue.

The true engine of her success has much to do with a remark Stewart makes in chapter one of her first book, the phenomenally successful *Entertaining* (1982):

> Entertaining provides a good excuse to put things in order (polish silver, wash forgotten dishes, wax floors, paint a flaking windowsill) and, sometimes, to be more fanciful or dramatic with details than usual. It is the moment to indulge in a whole bank of flowering plants to line the hall, or to organize a collection of antique clothes on a conspicuous coat-rack, or to try the dining-room table at an odd angle.

The second sentence, of course, is the stuff of a thousand jokes and parodies: not just a vase of flowers but a "bank" of them; the elaborate clothing display that no normal householder has the resources or the willingness to pull off. But the first sentence is the one to keep your eye on, with its unremarkable but attractive suggestion of a house put in order: a windowsill painted, floors gleaming under a new coat of wax. In the hundredth issue of *Martha Stewart Living*, Stewart says that she recently came across a memo she wrote at the magazine's inception, one that she feels expresses her vision as clearly today as it did then. "Our reader," the memo states, "still wants to iron, to polish silver, to set a sensible table, to cook good food."

She's right, of course. Millions of women still "want" to do these things, although an astonishing number of them (myself included) don't do much ironing or polishing anymore and are repeatedly frustrated by the nightly return to the kitchen. Our desire to reconnect with these tasks — which we fear are crucial to a well-run home — is commensurate with our uncertainty about what, exactly, they entail. Just as Disneyland presents a vision of Main Street USA that is very far afield from the real thing, so Stewart presents a vision of domesticity that involves as much make-believe as practicality, that is filled with allure and prettiness rather than the drudgery and exhaustion of which we are all so wary. She lectures not on the humdrum reality of sweeping the kitchen floor every night, but on the correct way to store two dozen specialty brooms. Not on washing the dishes meal after relentless meal, but on the advisability of transferring dishwashing liquid from its unattractive plastic bottle to a cut-glass cruet with a silver stopper. The Stewart fantasy encompasses the feminine interest in formal weddings and gracious entertaining, but principally — and more powerfully — it turns on a wistful and almost shameful attraction to ironing boards and newly washed crockery and good meals sensibly prepared. And on this wan longing, Stewart has built an empire.

What no biography of Stewart has yet accomplished is an insightful analysis of the core questions that her phenomenal success prompts. Many writers — especially male writers, such as Christopher Byron and Jerry Oppenheimer, the author of *Martha Stewart: Just Desserts* (1997) — have been fascinated by her famously mercurial temperament and the unsavory details of her personal life. But other than indulging in juicy speculation (such as Oppenheimer's creepy fascination with Stewart's heavy menstrual periods and Byron's notion that she had a hysterectomy as a form of birth control, a notion that only a man could believe and only a jerk could promulgate), they don't know what to do with these supposed secrets except to humiliate Stewart by making them public. The notion of an attractive late-midlife woman who offers homemaking advice on television but leads an off-camera life marked by nastiness and single-girl liberty is rife with comedic possibility (it is the basis for the Sue Ann Nivens character on *The Mary Tyler Moore Show*), and this type draws the cruelest of biographers. But these writers' books fail because they assume that Stewart's success is based on the stupidity of women, their inability to see through her many inconsistencies and hypocrisies. If only those dumb clucks would read the "Remembering" column more critically; they'd cancel their subscriptions in an instant! Her harshest critics miss nothing less than the heart of Stewart's appeal to women, the same thing that the feminists missed when they demonized housework: that women have a deeply felt emotional connection to housekeeping.

Feminists are dogged in their belief that liberated, right-on men will gladly share equally in domestic concerns, but legions of eligible men who enjoy nothing more than an industrious morning spent tidying the living room and laundering the dust ruffle have yet to materialize (and those men who do fit the bill tend not to be objects of erotic desire for hotshot young copywriters and cardiologists). If you want to make a feminist sputter with rage, remind her of those dark days in America's past when girls took home ec classes and boys took shop. But to watch yuppie parents squirm with dread and confusion when anything in their households goes on the fritz is to wonder whether it was such a bad thing for one half of the marriageable population to know how to mend a fallen hem and the other half to have rudimentary knowledge of the workings of a fuse box. And to see such people frantically dropping wads of cash on hanging shoe racks and designer closet organizers is to suspect that they don't even know where to look for what they've lost. Many Americans of substantial means live in houses in which the prospect of a hot home-cooked meal at the end of the day is dim, in which beds are left in a tangle of sheets and blankets rather than being properly aired and made each morning, in which a button popped off a shirt renders the shirt unwearable for weeks on end or quite possibly forever — because who has time to sew on a button? And who even knows how anymore? And let's not imagine what quarrel about gender-linked tasks the predicament might foment.

The book *Not Your Mother's Life* describes the arrangement New York literary agent Amy Lowe made with her husband: she would keep her high-powered job while he stayed home with the children. Yet she still had to do all the family laundry: "He'll throw a load in the washer where it sits all day," she moans, "or he'll leave it in the dryer so it's all wrinkled by the time I get home from work." Nor did the "folding lessons" she gave the man (surely a marital high point) do a lick of good. Browbeating one's mate into providing a higher standard of housework is, we've all come to agree, morally objectionable (see *The Feminine Mystique,* currently in its zillionth printing and still smokin' hot about the outlandish notion that one spouse might earn the money for a family's keep while the other provides the actual keep), so the stalemate established sometime in the midseventies remains.

All the quarrels and manifestos concerning the divvying up of housework (if this many people had spent this long discussing, say, the Battle of Thermopylae, they'd have left a record of infinitely greater variety and usefulness) have advanced the cause of housekeeping not at all. They have in fact made of housekeeping a lost art. It is this art that Cheryl Mendelson hopes to revive in this generation's most important book on the subject, *Home Comforts: The Art and Science of Keeping House.* She takes careful stock of the many unsuccessful ways in which people attempt to create homes that hark back to the standards and comforts of an earlier era: ways that include elaborate and costly interior decorating schemes or "nostalgic pastimes — canning, potting, sewing, making Christmas wreaths, painting china, decorating cookies" (an allusion, perhaps, to Stewart and the phenomenal success she has enjoyed promoting just such projects during the very years in which housekeeping has severely foundered). The most unsuccessful of these various approaches are overly rigorous home organization protocols, whose devotees "arrange their shoes along the color spectrum in a straight line and suffer anxiety if the towels on the shelf do not all face the same way," Mendelson writes. "They expend enormous effort on what they think of as housekeeping, but their homes often are not welcoming. Who can feel at home in a place where the demand for order is so exaggerated?"

Of housework, that hideous and reviled pastime (the "drudgery" of housework is the accepted description, as though the work still involved emptying chamber pots and wiping down bedposts with kerosene rags to ward off bedbugs), she writes, "Having kept house, practiced law, taught [in addition to a Harvard law degree, Mendelson holds a Ph.D. in philosophy], and done many other sorts of work, low- and high-paid, I can assure you that it is actually lawyers who are most familiar with the experience of unintelligent drudgery." In Mendelson's opinion, the widespread collapse of housekeeping explains a multitude of domestic woes: "Television often absorbs everyone's attention because other activities (such as music-making, letter-writing, socializing, reading, or cooking) require at least a minimum of foresight, continuity, order, and planning that the contemporary household cannot accommodate."

That her book is exhaustive is among its principal delights (my favorite chapter includes "a brief glance at the history of dusting"), but whether its prescriptions will engender noticeable change is highly debatable. (I confess that although I adore *Home Comforts,* I read it exactly as I often read cookbooks — straight through, enraptured, but finding no more of a call to immediate action than I found in *Bleak House* or *Our Man in Havana.*) How much easier it is to turn the pages of a Martha Stewart publication and make vague, unkept plans to scent the linen cupboard with handmade lavender sachets.

* * *

STEWART IS STERN and exacting about things for which
I have only the fondest and gentlest associations: flower
beds and freshly laundered clothes and home-cooked
food. That millions of people are happy to be lectured on
"family" and "tradition" by a woman whose own marriage imploded and whose relations with her only child
have been famously stormy used to drive me wild with
frustration. But lately I've softened on the old girl. She is
the producer of a myth about American family life that is
as old as Hollywood — and if we expected the men who
make our best-loved "family movies" to comport themselves honorably as husbands and fathers, we'd be sunk at
matinee time. Her faltering confessions about her private
domestic bewilderments (she should have "read more
psychology books," she has said about her early career as
a mother; it was "a big mistake" to have had an only child)
provide her most humanizing moments. And I find something touching and almost elegiac in her memories of the
family that raised her, for all the ridicule they receive: "We
all sat down to dinner at the same time, and we all got up
at the same time and we were very close-knit."

Clearly, something powerful is at work here, some
weaving together of the dream of a "close-knit" family with
rigid adherence to complicated baking and gardening

187

protocols. There was a time when the measure of a home was found in the woman who ran it — who was there all day long, who understood that certain aspects of "hominess" had less to do with spit and polish than with continuity and permanence. As these old standards wane, a new one has emerged, and it is Stewart's. No human effort is so fundamentally simple and pleasurable that she cannot render it difficult and off-putting (we are to be grateful that thus far she has not produced a marriage manual). But almost any project she cooks up is less daunting than the one it is meant to replace: keeping a family together, under one roof, home.

Clutter Warriors

SEVERAL YEARS AGO, during the psychically draining days following Christmas, I rolled a huge shopping cart into the home organization department of the Burbank Ikea and threw in so many baskets and boxes and under-bed storage units that my small son (who had been standing in the front of the cart, navigating) decided to clamber out, leaving just enough room for a big wicker hamper. We were there because the prospect of cleaning up the house after Christmas had struck me as unpleasant and oppressive, whereas the prospect of driving out to Burbank and eating a meatball lunch in the Ikea cafeteria had struck me as attractive and spirit-lifting. Best of all, we would not be shirking the work back home; we would be beginning it — or so I persuaded myself.

Like many women of my proximate age and social position (householders, mothers, irritable presiders over vast domestic holdings of Lego blocks and take-out menus and teetering stacks of unexamined shop-by-mail catalogues), I am preoccupied by clutter. Almost every domestic task seems to begin (and also to sputter out) in an effort to eliminate it, or at the very least to assign it to a well-chosen receptacle. This shared preoccupation has given rise to a wide host of American phenomena, only one of which is the Ikea home organization department.

The anticlutter movement is enormous, having spawned countless books, magazine articles (and actual magazines), videos, classes, and catalogues, as well as the 3,000-member-strong National Association of Professional Organizers. The "Eastern art" of feng shui is practiced in thousands of upscale, with-it households, and it proceeds from a "clear your clutter" premise. Anticlutter campaigns make for excellent voyeur sport. The visits to *Oprah* of the master organizer Julie Morgenstern are never disappointing. Sometimes Oprah has Morgenstern perform spot inspections of her employees' offices, events that offer superb moments of reality television: office doors swinging open in the manner of an FBI raid; shocked workers blinking into the camera lights, caught in flagrante with their overflowing mail crates and ripening piles of exercise clothes, their half-eaten lunches moldering on paper-strewn desktops.

Far more entertaining, however, are the home visits, which are not feared but highly coveted, and for which the competition is stiff. Viewers write long, importuning letters describing unabashedly the slovenly states of their homes, which they will gladly reveal to a national television audience if only Oprah will send them some help. If the winner is really lucky, Morgenstern herself will make a visit, bringing along her Hefty bags and plastic sorter baskets and brisk "nothing shocks me" professionalism. The houses are never squalid, but they are crammed with stuff — stuff that's been packed into drawers and cupboards and closets, no rhyme or reason to it, and not an inch of space to spare. No matter how big the kitchens are (and many of them are plenty big), they are never big enough, in part because the success of buy-in-bulk superstores has left people with an astonishing, pre-apocalyptic quantity of supplies. The video tour that begins each segment often reveals curious, forgotten outposts of spaghetti sauce or Formula 409 in the garage or beneath the stairs.

No matter what area of the house is under consideration (medicine cabinet, linen closet, kids' rooms), it is sure to be an absolute horror. In the old days, of course, this kind of general chaos would occasion a thorough spring-cleaning, with the children sent upstairs to clear out the mess underneath their beds and Dad dispatched to the garage under similar orders. But nowadays the home is foreign territory, a kind of very large hotel suite unintended for long-term habitation, and when the whole thing gets so overstuffed that it threatens to explode, the time has come to call in an expert.

The experts, Lord knows, are sympathetic to the psychological magnitude of tidying the house. *The Zen of Organizing*, which is studded with the inspirational words of boffo organizers from Plutarch to Martha Graham (although nothing at all from Joe Stalin, who by all accounts ran a very tight ship), begins with a description of how the author, Regina Leeds, sits with her clients, "calming" them before they open a single drawer: "We consciously leave fear and judgment behind." They also dress carefully and eat sensibly before beginning the work. Many authors of anticlutter books mention cluttering as a possible manifestation of obsessive-compulsive disorder, and it is not uncommon for them to discuss pharmaceutical approaches to dealing with a hall table heaped with *Pennysavers* and unsolicited AOL start-up disks. *Stop Clutter from Stealing Your Life,* by Mike Nelson, opens with a disclaimer: "I am not a professional organizer, psychologist, or psychiatrist," Nelson tells us in all earnestness, and his book (which is couched in the language of 12-step recovery programs) includes a chapter on "the medical view" of clutter and another on how clutter can disrupt a person's sex life, which goes far beyond the logistical problems posed by too many back issues of *Newsweek* fighting for space in the marriage bed.

Practitioners of the many home organization philosophies adhere to a few basic tenets. Central among them is the solemnly held belief that any possession, no matter how serviceable or expensive, that is stored unused and forgotten in a closet or a cupboard will eventually metastasize into clutter. Once this happens, there's hell to pay. The moment your stylish black-and-chrome cappuccino machine makes the terrible one-way crossing from "appliance" to "clutter," it stops simply occupying valuable shelf space and becomes an enemy within your home, capable of draining your energy, sapping your chi, interrupting your sleep, and generally bumming you out. Step one for the professional organizer is persuading the owner of said cappuccino maker to get rid of the thing before it causes real problems. This is often an uphill battle. For one thing, the owner may still be smarting over the twelve hundred clams she forked over to Williams-Sonoma for the really *good* cappuccino maker, the one with the energy-efficient standby mode.

Once she has been convinced of the need to chuck the thing, however, the method of disposal is almost irrelevant — although I'm often surprised, given how expensive many of these items are, at what short shrift the notion of hosting a garage sale gets. ("Ugh! Not worth it!" the Washington, D.C.–based organizer Jill Lawrence said when I broached the subject, telling me that garage sales make sense only if one is "on disability" and therefore broke, or new to the neighborhood and therefore lonely — a combination that stigmatizes the enterprise pretty effectively: GARAGE SALE SATURDAY: BROKE AND LONELY, EVERYTHING MUST GO.) Some disposal suggestions are peculiar in the extreme. "Take pictures of any items which are simply too bulky to store," recommends Harriet "The Miracle Worker" Schechter in her book *Let Go of Clutter,* and "then bid a fond adieu to the actual objects." It's a suggestion that would surely lead to some mighty odd conversations way down the road: "Hey, Granny, what's *this*?" "Why, that's a snapshot of my old standby-mode cappuccino maker, Johnny! Top of the line!"

Even more paralyzing than the prospect of letting go of one's expensive impulse purchases is the thought of hauling out and categorizing the thousand smaller things: the handfuls of half-sorted mail; the videotapes with and without their boxes; the reams of children's artwork; tangles of unmatched socks; outgrown Little Mermaid costumes; multiple packages of Imodium, most of them expired (the stockpiling and subsequent discovery and disposal of expired medications is a gold mine for drug companies); the birthday-cake candles and unspent Chuck E. Cheese's tokens and overdue notices from the library, all shoved into kitchen drawers — the whole miserable mess that is American family life as it is lived at a certain economic level. These debilitating decisions must be made one at a time, with the organizer instilling certain precepts in the client as they work. The professionals insist, for example, that householders designate a consistent "home" for each of their possessions, so that they don't end up with what Jill Lawrence calls "thirteen hammer syndrome," in which it becomes easier to haul ass down to the hardware store and buy a new hammer every time you need one than to spend a frustrating hour looking for an old one. ("But that's *obvious*," an acquaintance of mine said in disbelief when I explained this concept to him. "You'd be surprised," I told him.)

The organizers want clients to hew their household possessions down to the barest kit, augmented only by items of considered emotional or aesthetic value. Certainly only a masochist would object to Harriet Schechter's recommendation that one throw out one's Dear John letters and "hate mail," but there's a sense in many of these books that *any* kind of saving is inherently problematic, dysfunctional, bad. Judith Kolberg, the author of *Conquering Chronic Disorganization*, makes gentle fun of one of her clients, an elderly woman (the Greatest Generation tends to take a pounding in these books) who has saved margarine tubs for years. The woman's husband has tried to cure her by buying her a full set of Tupperware, and she has even "briefly sought counseling." But still she holds on to the tubs. She refuses to throw them in the recycling bin, for which I admire her. Recycling is one of the favorite quick fixes of the organizers, but of course the best way to recycle something — the method that depletes the fewest resources in the process — is simply to *use it again*, which of course necessitates saving it until a use presents itself. The resourceful Kolberg finds a charity that serves poor women and will be happy to take the tubs: "Welfare mothers are too poor to purchase Tupperware," she informs us, "and too thrifty to throw away leftovers." At last the old woman happily relinquishes most of her cache. The episode is presented as a triumph for the organizer (she got the clutter out of the house!), but of course it was really a triumph for the old woman, who knew instinctively that good plastic bowls with airtight lids ought not to be thrown out with the trash.

The sneaking suspicion I often get from reading such books is that the real purpose of cleaning out the closets is simply to make room for more stuff. Karen Kingston's best-selling *Clear Your Clutter with Feng Shui* tells the inspirational story of a woman who attended one of Kingston's workshops and got so fired up about a clutter-free life that she called Goodwill and said, "You are going to need to send a truck!" She "cleared out her ancient stereo system, stacks and stacks of junk, and all but five items of clothing from her wardrobe," thereby releasing "huge amounts of stuck energy, which created space for something new to come in." What exciting "new" thing would be coming? An unexplored talent? A zeal for charitable giving? No — more stuff! "A week later she received a check in the mail from her mother for $8,000, and she went straight out and bought herself a new sound system, a whole new wardrobe of wonderful clothes, and everything else she wanted."

Nowhere is this uneasy alliance between clutter-clearing and consumption more apparent than in the pages of *Real Simple* magazine, whose motto is "Do Less, Have More," with the editorial emphasis falling on the "Have More" part of the equation. To be fair, the magazine regularly makes gestures in the general direction of the simple life. A recent article revealing readers' responses to the question, "Which woman's life do you admire, and why?" featured a large black-and-white photograph of Dorothy Day, a cofounder of the Catholic Worker Movement: "Constantly surrounded by our society's desire to consume, she chose purposeful poverty."

Certainly this worthy woman would make an estimable role model for many people, but presumably not for most readers of *Real Simple,* which is filled to capacity with advertisements for luxury items, some of them garden-variety — six-burner stoves and Mercedes-Benzes and such — but many others of a highly specialized nature. There are regular ads for an American Standard bathtub of a remarkably silly design (it looks like a Shaker writing table into which a bathtub has crash-landed), which will set you back $1,400 but may not "simplify" your life as much as would taking a can of Comet to your old tub and making do with it. Almost every feature pitches one product or another, with purchasing information always included right up front. In essence *Real Simple* is a magazine about shopping; this is a fact that the advertisers embrace forthrightly. "Inspired by Shaker design," reads the copy on the bathtub ad, "not necessarily the lifestyle."

Each issue begins with a series of full-page "Simple Solutions" that tend to run along the following lines: "Simplify" your home exercise program by throwing out your free weights and buying stretch bands ($8) and a digital heart rate monitor ($50). "Simplify" your cleaning routine by dumping surface clutter into the Container Store's foldable mesh cubes ($3 to $12). "Simplify" your wine rack by (don't try to follow the logic here, or your brain will melt) "upgrading" its contents with $19 bottles of "rich Penfolds Old Vine Shiraz-Grenache-Mourvèdre," which (unlike the stretch bands and the mesh cubes) have the advantage of being unlikely to end up crammed into a closet, where — foster children of silence and slow time — they will surely turn into clutter, drain your energy, bum you out, screw up your sex life, and inspire you to write to Oprah begging for a bailout.

De-cluttering a household is a task that appeals strongly to today's professional-class woman. It's different from actual housework, because it doesn't have to be done every day. In fact, if the systems one implements are truly first-rate, they may stay in place for years. More appealing, the work requires a series of executive-level decisions. Scrubbing the toilet bowl is a bit of nastiness that can be fobbed off on anyone poor and luckless enough to qualify for no better employment. But only the woman of the house can determine which finger paintings ought to be saved for posterity, which expensive possessions ought to be jettisoned in the name of sleekness and efficiency.

·   ·   ·

A YEAR AFTER my Ikea trip (once the baskets and hampers had been filled with odds and ends, squirreled away, forgotten, and fermented into clutter), a friend came over and made a giggly confession: she had hired an organizer.

"How was it?" I asked, desperately curious.

"Great," she said, dreamily. "I'll give you her number." I called.

And so began one of the most important relationships in my life. My organizer, let us call her Sarah (for that is her name), has changed everything around here. In fact she's on retainer. We meet once a week. I have become absolutely obsessed with tidy closets, organized drawers, and clean vistas.

She comes over and we choose a project. There is never a shortage of things we could de-clutter and organize. (The boys' rooms are evergreen, and so are the kitchen countertops and the two writing tables in my office. We could do these projects every week.) I get a weird delight throwing things away. It is, literally, thrilling. I'm the daughter of Depression children; I was trained not to throw things out. I was brought up to believe that things should be mended and repaired. But with Sarah I throw things away, and instantly the house feels lighter and more spacious — and so do I. Almost every cupboard or drawer has something to be tossed — a towel that's lost its nap, a toy part long discarded, or an old invitation to some event or other.

Lately I've developed a reckless abandon toward it, tossing out notebooks without even looking in them, and whenever I do that, Sarah always says, "You're my favorite client."

In my mother's house, things — physical, actual things — were steadier. Objects could be relied upon to stay put. If something was acquired it wasn't going anywhere. The little Eiffel Tower my mother bought me at age six stayed on a certain bookshelf in a certain room for as long as I can remember. Ditto the miniature Indian drum from Yosemite and the six-inch hula girl, although she had a habit of making it upstairs to my bedroom and putting down stakes in the dollhouse.

A generation ago peaceful cohabitation with a certain amount of clutter was possible, because so many other aspects of home life were ordered and regular. Perhaps only those of us old enough to have grown up in houses in which the old ways were observed — in which dinner was eaten in the dining room, care was taken not to track dirt on good carpets, and wet towels were not left to sour — know what is missing from so many homes today. The current upper-middle-class practice of outsourcing even the most intimate tasks may free up valuable time for an important deposition, but it by no means raises the caliber of one's home life. My children attended a rather soignée Los Angeles preschool, whose élan was once jeopardized by an outbreak of head lice. Parents were given brochures for a service that takes care of the problem in one's home. This seemed a more attractive prospect than spending a morning combing for nits. But on reflection, having someone come to my home to delouse my children seemed perilously close to having someone (presumably not the same person) come in and service my husband on nights when I'd rather put on my flannel nightie and watch *Dateline NBC*. There's a point at which you have to suit up and do the job yourself. Otherwise family members start to wonder whether they're living in a home or in a sort of lawless, anything-for-hire (albeit well-appointed) Bangkok flophouse.

What's missing from so many affluent American households is the one thing you can't buy: the presence of someone who cares deeply and principally about that home and the people who live in it; who is willing to spend a significant portion of each day thinking about what those people are going to eat and what clothes they will need for which occasions; who knows when it's time to turn the mattresses and when the baby needs to be taken out for a bit of fresh air and sunshine. Because I have no desire to be burned in effigy by the National Organization for Women, I am impelled to say that this is work Mom *or* Dad could do, but in my experience women seem to have more of a connection to the work — and to the way that it should be done — than men do. Clearing clutter has become a substitute for something many women miss and detest: housekeeping at its most basic and humdrum.

For many modern women, myself included, thrashing through the flotsam of a household in the cheerful company of a professional organizer provides the illusion that we are getting control of the lives we are living.

To Hell with All That

> This is one of those moments in which the interests of mothers are seen to diverge sharply from the wishes of daughters.
>
> — JOAN DIDION, *Democracy*

THROUGHOUT MY CHILDHOOD, the thirty-five-cent Cardinal edition of Dr. Spock sat on a kitchen counter beside another font of domestic good counsel, *"The Settlement" Cook Book*. The books have fallen into my hands now, their spines mended with tape, their pages buckling with age. To this day, the two homely volumes (decommissioned and reclassified as mementos) are capable of a profound act of evocation — of my mother, certainly, but more powerfully of the qualities she once represented to me: competence, benevolence, calm authority. To be a child in those days and to have a mother who possessed those two books — and the cheerful willingness to read them and to follow their practical and time-honored suggestions — was to live in a world that seems to me now a bygone age, as remote and unrecoverable as Camelot: a world of good meals turned out in orderly fashion, of fevers cooled without a single frantic call to the pediatrician, of clothes mended and repaired and pressed back into useful service rather than discarded to the rag heap as soon as a button pops or a sleeve unravels.

If a household is a tiny state, as of course it is, then my mother was the unquestioned potentate of ours — her command unchallenged, our fealty unwavering — although rarely a vociferous one. (If, while wandering through the kitchen, I caught sight of her cooking dinner, I would not have taken any more note of her than I did of the humming refrigerator or the shining toaster. It was her absences I noticed, but she was not often absent.) To be one of her subjects was to be assured of safety, continuity, comfort of the highest order. God was in his heaven, and a rump roast was in the oven, seasoned with salt, pepper, and ginger, and basted with fat from the pan.

This was a long time ago, or so it seems to me now, although I am not old or even far into middle age. This was before housewifery was understood to be an inherently oppressive state, before a marriage soured was a marriage abandoned; this was in the time when thrift and economy were still the cornerstones of middle-class American life. It was a rare night that the whole family ate dinner in a restaurant; "convenience" foods consisted of Swanson frozen dinners, their aluminum trays saved for all eternity (for mixing up four colors of poster paint for a bored child; for catching a drip from a leaking roof). They were called TV dinners then, but in my experience they were not eaten in front of the television. They were eaten — convivially and with gusto — in the dining room: place mats, folded napkins, glasses to the right of knives. In my childish apprehension of things, my father was happiest when he was sitting in his armchair reading a big, fat book, and my mother when she was standing at her ironing board transforming a chaotic basket of wash into a set of sleek and polished garments.

Which is why it came as such a shock to me when my mother suddenly pulled the plug on the whole operation. It was 1973; I was twelve. The story, as she always told it: One morning she cooked breakfast for my father and me and sent us on our way (a scramble for lunch box and briefcase, the daily struggle to get my hair brushed and braided, two sets of feet stumping down the front steps, and then — quiet). The morning was hers, and she had big plans for it. She filled a basin with warm, soapy water, set it on the utility ledge of the kitchen stepladder, and climbed up. Her intention was to wash down the wallpaper, of which she was rather fond (it had a cheerful blue and white pattern with a Dutch motif; she had hung it herself). But standing on the ladder, dripping sponge in hand, something happened. In one clear moment, staring at a little windmill or a tiny Dutch girl, it became no longer possible for her to go on living that particular life anymore. I would have been just arriving at school; my father would have been getting off the bus at the bottom of Euclid Avenue, headed for the English department and his morning class. My sister would have been making her way to the high school, and the fogs and mists that settle on the Berkeley Hills every night would have been just lifting when my mother threw the sponge back in the basin and said — out loud, to no one but herself, and apparently with finality — "To hell with it." And then she climbed off the ladder.

It must have been a bleak moment. She would have sat down at the kitchen table and lit a cigarette with trembling hands. Whiskey, the wirehaired terrier, would have been hovering solicitously close by, confused by the outburst. And all the while she was apparently looking around the homey little kitchen — my favorite room of the house! location of bacon sandwiches and homemade root beer and apple betties, warm from the oven — and suddenly seeing it for what it was: the center of her working life. The place where she turned out meal after meal and washed the same dishes and pots over and over again, and waited around, with her books and her cigarettes, for everyone to come home. And so, in one fateful, life-changing declaration, she suited words to feelings — To hell with it! — and went off to look for the want ads.

But to hell with *what* exactly? This was the question that plagued me for many unhappy months after the stepladder resolution. In the first place, I realize now, to hell with the demoralizing nature of make-work cleaning projects. And to hell with wasting her education. Hadn't she sailed through nursing school on a sea of A's? Wasn't she still consulted about ailments and remedies by half the people she knew? But most important was this: to hell with her marriage — or at least with its most unpleasant aspect, my father's cheapness and my mother's absolute lack of financial power.

My mother could stretch a dollar as well as anyone. She was a Depression child who ran the household according to the penny-saving mottoes of the time: "Eat it up, use it up, wear it out, or go without." We rarely ate dinner in restaurants, we all squawked as one when we heard that someone had spent an outrageous sum of money for something, we shared a messianic faith in a cobbler's power to transform a pair of scuffed shoes into something worthy of a Saturday night. We were the unembarrassed owners of a secondhand clothes dryer, a used electric can opener, and two student desks hauled home from a campus rummage sale for five bucks a pop. (I can still remember rushing down to campus with my parents — cups of tea abandoned on the kitchen table, jackets jostled onto shoulders as we hurried to the car — as soon as my mother came across a newspaper notice of the sale.)

But by the time my mother reached midlife, she longed for things that weren't worn or secondhand. She wanted decent furniture for the family room, a new deck, and (bless her heart) something for me: a wall. My bedroom was nothing more than a wide spot in the upstairs hall that led to the shared bathroom. She wanted to build a wall so that I might really have a room. She also wanted to take me to Disneyland, where all of my friends had been several times. But my father wouldn't allow her to buy or to do any of these things. She was stuck. He earned the money, and he had the final say on how it was spent. To hell with it.

He said he wouldn't allow her to work. She told him to drop dead. Two weeks later, she was once again a working woman for the first time in seventeen years.

She was nervous about going back to nursing after so many years away from it, but a health insurance company in San Francisco was eager to hire RN's as medical claims adjusters. She bought some drip-dry pants suits and half a dozen Ship 'n Shore blouses in pretty colors; she bought a BART commuter ticket and studied the route map. The Sunday afternoon before she started, she went into the kitchen and made five casseroles and stacked them in the freezer. She left defrosting instructions under a magnet on the refrigerator door, and when I got up Monday morning, she was gone.

Almost as soon as my mother began working, she cheered up. The glooms and sulks that had so often descended upon her lifted miraculously. (Wretched little egomaniac that I was, I hadn't taken any note of them until they vanished.) For my mother, a return to paid work was a return to how she saw herself at the deepest level. She was someone who took care of other people — it was woven into the fabric of her being as tightly as my father's need to be taken care of was woven into his. But once her children began to grow up, and her husband's job required ever more hours of him, she was increasingly finding herself out of work in her own home. There were people who needed her care, but they didn't spend their days at 22 Bret Harte Road.

My sister was planning her escape to college and was more or less untroubled by my mother's return to work. My father had no choice but to put up with the decision. I alone of all the household was truly miserable. To my thinking, my mother's change of heart constituted child abandonment, plain and simple. "Being home alone is stressful for a child," psychologist David Elkind has written, and he's dead right. Just walking through the front door each afternoon to be met by the quiet gloom of the empty living room was depressing. On my first day as a latchkey child, I lost the key. A key was hidden under a stone for me, but I used it once and forgot to return it. It vanished immediately. Frustrated, my mother tied a third key on a piece of thick white string and hung it around my neck, a weighty reminder that I'd been dumped by Mom. The big pots of geraniums by the front door went to seed; the breakfast dishes were often still on the table at three o'clock in the afternoon; when the teacher asked whose mother might chaperone a field trip, I kept my hands folded on my desk and burned with disappointment and shame.

Afternoons alone in the house were often frightening. It did not help that I am a hysteric by nature. When Patty Hearst was kidnapped across town, I became convinced I was next. We had so much in common — blue eyes and brown hair, terry-cloth bathrobes, Catholic girlhoods. That her father was one of the richest men in California and mine was a college professor with a mortgage and a car loan were details that did not factor into my threat assessment. Still, in the early seventies in Berkeley, there were plenty of bad things happening on a more random basis. One day there was a knock at our front door, the top half of which was a big, swing-out window. I opened the window to two young men who were standing on our porch and whose question to me (I can't now recall it) was so obviously trumped up, whose interest was so clearly in the living room beyond me, that I swung the window shut midsentence and locked it. I stood watching from behind a curtain as they made their way up the street, knocking on doors and peering through windows until they were out of sight. I reported the incident to my parents, who advised me not to let my imagination run wild.

My terror of kidnappers and burglars eventually reached such a pitch that my mother — who had by then left the insurance company and returned to nursing, taking a job at a convalescent hospital — arrived at a novel solution to the problem, one that anticipated by twenty years both on-site day care and Take Our Daughters to Work Day. She bought a couple of yards of blue and white ticking, ran up a candy striper uniform on the sewing machine, and introduced me, at age thirteen, to a career in the health-care industry. In lieu of a lunch hour, she would leave the hospital at three o'clock, pick me up from school, and take us both back to work to finish the shift. I would change out of my school uniform into my work clothes and spend the afternoon officiously copying chart head-ings, wheeling patients around the facility (a courtesy they tended to endure rather than appreciate), and making an endless series of tongue-depressor houses and cotton-ball bunnies in the day room, where I was encouraged in my work by the young, friendly occupational therapist.

I did not last long in my new post. I tended to grow bored long before quitting time, and it was hard for my mother to do her job and also put up with my endless pes-tering that we knock off early and swing by McDonald's for shakes. Eventually she took an even better job at a hospital in Oakland, which was too far away for her to nip out and pick me up each afternoon, putting an end to the program for good. Once again I was on my own, letting myself into the house through either the front door or an unlocked window, finding some kind of snack in the kitchen (the defrosting casserole would be sitting unappetizingly on the counter in a puddle of melt), and fretting about unseen dangers.

It is almost impossible for me to imagine a middle-class mother today doing what mine did then — going to work and making absolutely no provisions for her school-age child, other than to tie a key around her neck and hope for the best. Those are the kinds of plans that these days are usually made by women who have no choice but to work and who must accept whatever hardship comes along with the deal. They are not the plans of a woman who goes to work for the excitement and diversion it offers.

My mother was by no means indifferent about me; I was her pet, the baby of the family. But back then children were not under constant adult supervision, even if their mothers were housewives. By the time I was five, I was allowed to wander away from the house as long as I didn't cross any big streets. I had the run of the neighborhood at six. So the fact that I would be home alone in the afternoons at the advanced age of twelve was not a radical or overly worrisome one to my mother. A good friend of mine was only nine when her mother chewed her leg out of the trap, heading off to a volunteer job at a home for the retarded and leaving the child on her own in the afternoons. Such an arrangement was not then seen as a shocking dereliction of duty. A nine-year-old could be trusted with a key; a nine-year-old knew how to work a telephone if anything went wrong.

Moreover, anxiety as a precondition of the maternal experience had not yet been invented. We kids were topped up with Salk vaccine, our fathers had saved the world, and our neighborhoods were chock-full of busybody housewives who delighted in scolding other people's errant children. Terrible things happened then, just as they do today. But they tended not to have the titanic significance of the contemporary event. Once, when I was in third grade, we were all given purple and white mimeographed letters to bring home to our mothers. The letters reported that a child molester had been preying on children walking home from the next elementary school over. "What's a child molester?" I kept asking my mother, who stood in the kitchen reading the letter in a concerned way. "What's a child molester?" That was not for me to know, but neither was it cause for my mother to forbid me from roaming around the neighborhood after school. I should just "be careful." ("Careful of *what?*" Just careful.) My mother and her friends probably would not have made a bestseller of *The Lovely Bones.*

The second factor dissuading my mother from staying

home with me was that, at age twelve, I wasn't doing much that required her presence. The notion that after-school hours might constitute prime time for enrichment and improvement — athletic, academic, social, psychiatric — was still years away. To have been a child of the American suburbs thirty years ago was to spend much of your time nearly driven mad by boredom. It was the engine of the very mischief and high jinks that we remember most fondly. When I think of what it was like to be a girl in the sixties, I remember an endless series of afternoons, each an ungraspable piece of time. I watched television, cheated death on my Schwinn, and lifted up rocks looking for pill bugs. In those days children didn't have "passions" and "talents"; we had hobbies and collections — glass animals and plastic horses for girls, baseball cards for boys, and stamps for geeks of both genders. These were activities that required no parental involvement and that produced just as little quantifiable enrichment. Why should my mother have to sulk around the kitchen weepy with frustration, her only job to provide me with a beacon of reassurance — and to muscle off the Symbionese Liberation Army if they came for me — while I wrestled the cats into pinafores and watched reruns of *Lost in Space*?

Besides, the rhetoric of liberation didn't exhort women to go to work in spite of their children, but, at least partly, because of them. The notion was that housewives made poor mothers. Betty Friedan reported a "strange new problem" with those children "whose mothers are always there, driving them around, helping with homework — an inability to endure pain or discipline or pursue any self-sustained goal of any sort, a devastating boredom with life." Being on my own recognizance was supposed to toughen me up, to deliver me from my mother's crippling cosseting and vault me to new levels of independence — not an unreasonable theory. If I had a different temperament, it might have worked. (As it is, however, I remain an inveterate loser of keys and sunglasses and credit cards, and my anxiety about being alone in a house borders on the pathological.) A well-known 1970 position paper on day care by Louise Gross and Phylis Taube Greenleaf called the institution essential for "the liberation of children." For what were the tots learning at home except that it was a place of female enslavement?

•   •   •

MY MOTHER'S TENURE as a working woman was short-lived. We spent a year overseas on sabbatical — requiring my mother to give up the best job of the lot — and by the time we returned, my father had reinvented himself as a successful late-life novelist, a turn of events that energized and occupied them both. She was happy enough to ac-company him on book tours and publishing events, a combination of glamorous literary wife and girl Friday. But I always guiltily assumed that it was partly my whining and balking that was responsible for her giving up. She and I were exceedingly close — "enmeshed," I believe, is the term now in vogue — and although I was the only one in the household who hated her job, I was the only one who really understood what it meant to her. Like most marriages, hers traded interludes of excitement with long stretches of tedium, and as an adult I have often thought of how much better off my mother would have been if she'd had a job — money of her own, power of her own — as she faced them.

Thirty years later the world has changed. The notion of a woman being blindsided by the stultification of housekeeping is positively quaint. We've been so thoroughly indoctrinated about the politics of housework that we can hardly scrape a dish without fuming about the inequitable distribution of domestic labor within a marriage. What has also changed is the role that the income of middle-class working mothers plays in family finances. When my mother returned to work, the engine of our family's financial machine had already been constructed. My father's income paid the mortgage, the car note, the taxes; it paid for groceries and doctor bills and clothes. None of my mother's new money would need to be diverted to the expenses of running a household. Furthermore, my parents had old-fashioned beliefs about money, beliefs that left my mother free to spend her earnings on whatever she wanted. One of my father's objections to her working was that it was emasculating to have a working wife. Worse still would be taking any of her money.

Today's career mom is often trying to make partner or become regional sales manager or executive editor, jobs that require a tremendous number of hours and a willingness to allow urgent appeals, via BlackBerry or cell phone, to interrupt even the best-laid plans for family time. And all the while, breathing down their necks, unwilling to give an inch, are the women who have chosen to stay home. They've given up on the power and autonomy of work for one signal reason: to ensure that their children get the very best of themselves. And every day they're raising the stakes and the standards on what is required to be a good mother.

These, of course, are the tensions of our times. To call them a preoccupation among the mothers I know would be to commit a grave act of understatement. Last year I attended a fund-raiser for the Los Angeles nursery school that my sons attended. It was a dinner dance with an auction, and the chief items up for bid were chairs hand-painted by the members of each class, a project that had been laboriously created and supervised by an exceedingly earnest and energetic at-home mother. She was at the podium, a little drunk and flushed with pride about the furniture, the decorating of which she was describing in effusive and somewhat agitated terms. Leaning against a far column watching her, with drinks in hands and sardonic half smiles on their faces, were two of my friends: a lawyer and a movie producer. I was propelled toward them the way I was once propelled toward the cool girls in high school. And I suddenly had the bona fides to join them: my writing had recently begun to be published. I sidled up; they made room. We looked at the woman: think of all she'd sacrificed to stay home with her children; think of the time she'd spent dipping our own precious children's hands in paint so that they could press their little prints on the miniature Adirondack chairs. "Get a life," one of us said, and we all giggled and drank some more. And then we turned our backs on the auction and talked about work.

But I'm craven enough to change colors if the occasion calls for it. "Is that poor child's mother *ever* at school?" someone hissed when a (perfectly happy) little girl marched off with her nanny one recent afternoon. "*I've* never seen her," I clucked back, feeling guilty about knifing the absent mother and glad as hell I hadn't sent my own nanny to pick up the boys that day.

The tiresome question of whether or not women ought to stay home with their children has become the stuff of an endless, fruitless debate framed around the assumption that with enough talk, talk, talk (the woman's cure-all), the correct solution to the puzzle can be divined and the whole subject laid to rest. "What's better for a child," women's magazines forever ask, "if a bad mother stays home or if a good mother works and then spends important time with her children?" It is a query that reminds me of the type of hypothetical questions posed in Philosophy 101 or a rousing game of Scruples — and with just as little ultimate usefulness. (What if the bad mother also happens to be a rotten surgeon?) That there now exists a nationwide "mommy war," a great Mexican standoff between the working and nonworking mothers of the middle and upper-middle classes, is a simplification of a complex situation, but not an entirely inaccurate one.

When my twin sons were born seven years ago, there was no question where I stood on all of this: I was certain that it was better for children — much better — if their mothers stayed home with them, which is exactly what I did. (I cannot, however, claim a whit of self-sacrifice: I was home anyway, plugging away at unpublishable short stories, an activity I was only too happy to abandon.) Each long afternoon that I spent in the backyard, watching the little boys poke at things with sticks and roll their cars and wagons down the driveway to the big black gates, was an investment of sorts, the value of which would be revealed when they got to nursery school. There, I imagined, the children would fall into two easily recognizable camps: the wan and neurotic kids of working mothers, and the emotionally robust, confident kids of stay-at-home moms. What a bust. There was no difference at all that I could divine. If anything, the kids of the working mothers seemed a little more on the ball. My boys (whose experience of life to that point had involved being endlessly catered to by risibly besotted late-life parents) would drop their sweaters and toys on the playground and forget they existed, while their friends whose mothers worked took care of their own things, putting sweaters in cubbies, keeping track of toys and shoes. Many of the children of the working mothers sailed into the classroom without a backward glance; they were used to not having their mothers beside them. They looked, in fact, as if they were ready to take over the world.

In the end, what did my boys gain from those thousand days they spent with me before school took them out into the larger world? Nothing, it seems to me, of any quantifiable value. No head start in life that will ensure them of some prize that will forever elude the children of working mothers. All they gained, really, was the sweetness of being with the person who loved them most in the world. All they gained was an immersion in the most powerful force on earth: mother love. And perhaps there is something of worth in that alone.

Support for this opinion was readily at hand in my mother's kitchen. For even when she was off in San

Francisco evaluating medical claims, the Cardinal edition of Dr. Spock was sitting there on the shelf, and it contained some sensible, humane, and insightful words on the subject. Feminists have been roasting Dr. Spock on a slow spit for decades now, and they show no sign of letting up, even though he died in 1998 and long ago surrendered without a fight his position as America's foremost child care expert. Indeed, the section titled "Working Mothers" might well inflame such women if only for its placement in the book: it is included in a dire final chapter called "Special Problems." In those unreconstructed days, to have a working mother landed you in the same unlucky category as the Handicapped Child and the Premature Baby. But when I read his actual words on the subject (the infamous section is hardly four pages long), I find in them the most sympathetic accounting of the complexities of this kind of motherhood I've ever encountered.

Spock identifies three varieties of the species. "Some mothers *have* to work to make a living," the section begins sensibly enough. "It doesn't make sense to let mothers go to work making dresses in factories or tapping typewriters in offices and have them pay other people to do a poorer job of bringing up their children." His solution? The government "should pay a comfortable allowance to all mothers (of young children) who would be otherwise compelled to work." Exactly the program many of them are currently demanding. A second type of working mother: "A few mothers, particularly those with professional training, feel that they must work because they wouldn't be happy otherwise. I wouldn't disagree if a mother felt strongly about it, provided she had an ideal arrangement for her children's care. After all, an unhappy mother can't bring up very happy children." Again, I can hardly imagine a comment less likely to antagonize a feminist.

"What about the mother who doesn't absolutely have to work," he asks, "but [who] would prefer to, either to supplement the family income, or because they think they will be more satisfied themselves and therefore get along better at home? That's harder to answer." His response to that thorny question lies in one of the most compelling appeals for full-time motherhood I've ever read:

> The important thing for a mother to realize is that the younger a child, the more important it is for him to have a steady, loving person taking care of him. In most cases the mother is the best one to give him this feeling of "belonging," safely and surely. She doesn't quit on the job, she doesn't turn against him, she isn't indifferent to him. . . . If a mother realizes clearly how vital this kind of care is to a small child, it may make it easier for her to decide that the extra money she might earn, or the satisfaction she might receive from an outside job is not so important after all.

Obviously he's right about a mother being uniquely suited for the full-time care of her children. What more persuasive argument could there be than his simple and moving description of the maternal bond? What he could not have predicted was that such a huge number of women would fall into his second category. Mothers with professional training are thick on the ground these days, and their desire to work is at once more complex and more profound than the great man imagined. To be a woman with an education and a desire to take part in the business of the world — to have a public life only one-thousandth as vital and exciting as Dr. Spock's — yet to have one's days suddenly dwindle to the simple routines of child care can handily diminish what is best and most hard-fought in a person. It isn't simply a matter of "extra money" or "satisfaction." For many women the decision to abandon — to some extent — either their children or their work will always be the stuff of grinding anxiety and uncertainty, of indecision and regret.

●   ●   ●

IN MY MOTHER'S blue and white kitchen, there was a china plate on which was painted the legend A GOOD MOTHER MAKES A HAPPY HOME. And in the old Bonwit Teller bandbox that contained my dress-up clothes were

the totems of her romantic youth: silk dresses and specta-
tor pumps, and outrageous hats, some with netted veils.
In its own box — very important, although looking a little
like a cupcake — was her old Bellevue cap, awarded to her
on the day she had earned her RN. So this was my mother,
someone whose life contained multitudes — romance, and
work, and now her own principality: 22 Bret Harte Road.

It was enough to stake my future on, a set of
expectations — beauty and glamorous work in youth,
industrious household management in the years that
followed — that I could dream about for hours, whether
I was running my little Hoover vacuum over the living
room carpets or clacking across the sunporch in stilettos.
My work, my career — did anyone even bother to say this
aloud? — would be a short-term proposition, lasting only
as long as it took to meet Mr. Right. How naturally and
easily that would happen, and how powerfully he would
be drawn to me, granting me both my own principality
and a full-size Hoover. There was everything to look forward to. A woman's life, I once innocently believed, un-
folded in a series of epochs, each ending cleanly as the
next began.

When my mother died, I gave a maudlin eulogy about
all the days we spent together when I was small, shopping
at Hink's department store and eating peeled apricots
and lying down for naps in the big bed under the gable

window of her bedroom. I probably should have found something more estimable to say about her, but in the days after her death all I could think about was what a wonderful thing it had been to be raised at home, by a mother who loved me.

My Life without You

Goodnight stars
Goodnight air
Goodnight noises everywhere
— MARGARET WISE BROWN,
Goodnight Moon

MY MOTHER DIED the way Mike lost his money in *The Sun Also Rises:* very slowly and then all at once. I had been with her two weeks before, and any fool could have seen that she was near the end. But she was my mother; I thought she was going to live forever.

Afterward, in the hospital, they gave me a white plastic bag of her clothes, but I must have set it down somewhere and left it behind. On the sidewalk my hands were empty, but there was no turning back. My father and I were in haste to get to the mortuary. The moment of death had uncorked something in us, transformed the catatonia of the vigil into momentum. We were talking fast, and then we were driving fast, and at the mortuary we didn't sit down in the waiting room; we paced it. We were eager to stay one step ahead of things, to keep the situation under control. Only my sister fully grasped what had happened. She stayed with the body until the attendants from the hospital morgue arrived for it. She thanked the nurses and said good-bye to them. She understood that the end had come.

I couldn't wait for the memorial service, which we held a month later, in my parents' house. It wasn't until the event was in full swing, with people drinking our wine and talking about any old thing — the rains, the *London Review of Books*, the Republicans — that I realized we had not gathered to summon her; we had gathered to begin forgetting her.

I slipped up the stairs, away from the crowd, and sat on the floor of my mother's dressing room, the way I used to sit underneath the ironing board or the kitchen table when I was small and I wanted to be near her. The windows were open, and a breeze was stirring the silk blouses and scarves. Her dressing gown was on the peg where she had left it the morning she had been taken away in the ambulance. All her shoes were lined up; I could take any pair I wanted. I could take any sweater, any coat. She was never coming back.

I was a grown woman with a husband, children, a household of my own to manage. Nothing untoward had happened. There was cause only for maturity, forbearance, and sadness. I was old enough to take care of myself.

The thing to do was to go downstairs, accept compliments on my smart black skirt, and talk about the *London Review of Books*.

The thing to do was to let the wound heal over.

January 10, 2003

It is early in the afternoon, and I am standing in my kitchen thinking about two things: that it has been two years, exactly, since my mother's death, and that I have forgotten to buy a jar of pitted black olives.

The first fact is remarkable. It has now been indisputably proven that what she told me all my life, to my adamant disbelief, is true: I miss her, but I don't need her anymore.

On the other hand, I really do need the olives. They're called for in the recipe I'm cooking, which comes out of a book titled *One Dish Suppers* that I bought a week ago with the hope that it will solve the nightly dinner crisis by introducing radical simplicity into the routine. I've even committed myself to assembling the casseroles (we've had two so far — one bland, the other vile) midday to keep the evening from feeling rushed. But now production must be stopped: no olives. I'm due in Beverly Hills in an hour; afterward I'll stop at Ralphs. I put the casserole in the fridge, kiss the children, and ask the babysitter to tidy the kitchen. I'm off.

I'm driving on Santa Monica Boulevard and just passing the gilded minarets of the Beverly Hills city hall when I say, out loud and as though addressing someone else, "Maybe the anniversary of your mother's death isn't the best day to get a mammogram."

Ridiculous! It was my mother who had truck with superstition, omens, vague warnings. Not me. Besides, she died of old age and bad lungs, not cancer. Onward, and then to Ralphs.

The form on the clipboard is reassuring: Did your mother ever have breast cancer? Grandmother? Sister? Aunt? No. I carry the genetic markers for all kinds of female complaints — mild hysteria, bouts of sadness, migraine — but not cancer. Let's get this over with — the olives!

The technician is newly engaged and planning a big wedding. She wants to go to Hawaii for her honeymoon, and I talk to her somewhat frantically about hotels in Maui. (My tone is induced by nudity and embarrassment, not fear.)

I'm told to wait before getting dressed, and then I'm told that the doctor wants a second set of films, and then that he wants a sonogram — and none of this scares me. I have recently accompanied two of my best friends to sonograms ordered after worrisome mammograms. The sonogram, I have learned, is a painless prelude to immediate and complete relief. It precedes a dinnertime glass of wine with one's husband — the children unaware of what has almost befallen them — followed by a return to the newly blessed routine and exhaustion of the everyday.

But then a funny thing happens. Dr. Klein — a kibitzer, a wisecracker — comes into the room, and he looks grave. I ask about his sons, but he hardly listens to me. And then he says a bad word: *shadow*.

The technician is in the room with us, and I see that her attention has clearly shifted from her Hawaiian honeymoon to me and my situation. Her workday has taken an interesting turn. We begin.

The thing to do is to keep Dr. Klein talking, make him laugh. He likes me: I sent him a baby announcement when the twins were born; my husband's uncle is the headmaster of the school his boys attend. He won't let anything bad happen to me.

And then he says, "It's in the sonogram."

"Should I have a biopsy?" ("No, no, no," he will say, and "Let's just keep an eye on it for the next few months.")

But instead he says, "Yes, a needle biopsy."

The need to get out of the darkened room is suddenly urgent, and I start to struggle up in my paper gown. "When should I schedule that?"

He puts a hand on my chest and pushes me gently back down toward the hard table. "We're going to do it right now."

Suddenly I see that the technician — betrayer! — has been quietly sliding instruments out of sealed white paper envelopes, and she passes them on a steel tray to Dr. Klein.

The pain is sharp and sudden, a blessing: pure distraction.

Afterward I shake so badly that he doesn't want to let me leave the office, or even to stand up from the table, but I have to get away from him.

And then, to keep me in the room a little longer, he begins talking in an animated way about breast cancer. Specifically the Avon breast cancer walk and how I have to remember how many thousands of women go on those walks.

"They couldn't have a pancreatic cancer walk!" He's giving a pep talk, I can hear it in his tone and cadence, if not in his words. "Almost no one survives pancreatic cancer."

Survives?

•   •   •

ON THE SIDEWALK outside his office I feel as though I've escaped from a rapist or a murderer. My breast is throbbing, and there's gauze taped to it to catch the blood. A thirty-minute appointment has taken more than two hours. Why hasn't anyone come looking for me? It's getting dark, and the street is jammed with traffic.

When I was in the office, all I could think about was calling my husband. But now, with the cell phone at last in my hand, I no longer want to. I don't want anyone to know what just happened to me in that building. Like anything shameful, it needs to be kept secret. And besides, I don't want my husband right now. I want my mother. For the first time, two years after watching her die, I realize — I truly understand, to the marrow of my bones — that I have lost her.

I put the phone in my purse and head toward the parking garage.

It's rush hour, and I sit in the car with my wounded breast and inch along Wilshire Boulevard. I feel like a woman who has just begun an affair. No one knows about the two hours of intimacy and violence that I have shared with another man. The gauze pad on my breast is incriminating; it's like damp underwear after a tryst. It will give me away.

I'm stuck opposite the Beverly Hills Saks when the phone rings, and I turn down the radio and answer it. My husband is calling to say hello.

"Did Dr. Klein call you?" I ask.

"What? No." And then he remembers. "Did you have your mammogram today?"

"I have breast cancer," I say, and now it has begun.

233

●   ●   ●

AT EACH STEP down the ladder into the new place, there is only bad news. The mammogram that is supposed to rule out cancer has confirmed it. The chest X-ray that was supposed to put the worst fears to rest has come back revealing its own suspicious mass, this one in my right lung. The surgery to remove what is expected to be a small tumor produces a large one. The pathology report tells that I have a particular kind of breast cancer — one distinguished by overexpression of the HER2/neu gene — that is known to be especially aggressive and cunning. A second surgery brings more news: the cancer is not contained in my breast; it has begun leaking through my lymphatic system.

At a certain point I begin to understand: I'm not sick. I'm dying.

●   ●   ●

DEATH SEEMED BETTER than what they had planned for me: chemotherapy, which would make me bald and weak and ruined; radiation; hormone therapy to dry up any bit of womanhood left behind; and then — "unsex me now" — they would take my ovaries and uterus. There was even one especially ghoulish doctor eyeing one last choice

234

bit: my cervix. It seemed like a moment to cut my losses. *"Do not resuscitate!"* I'd screamed at all the doctors two nights before my mother died. She was unsentimental and certain, and she hated indignity. I could follow her.

Wherever she was — even if it was nowhere and darkness and the end of things — I could go, too.

The boys would turn five on February 5. It was their golden birthday. They were small. They needed me.

I stayed.

• • •

ALMOST AS SOON as I offered up my body to them, the doctors began to take mercy on me. The shadow in my lungs turned out to be nothing more than a scar left over from an old pneumonia. The lymph nodes were indeed "involved," but perhaps not fatally — a clutch of them were excised, and only one was cancerous. My chances of survival were reconfigured. My head was shaved; a port was embedded in my chest wall so that the poison could be mainlined into me with maximum efficiency. The nurses in my oncologist's office warmed up to me. I seemed someone worth getting to know, someone who was going to be hanging around for a while.

The binder in the surgeon's office with the tabbed section called "Getting Your Affairs in Order" became merely a binder filled with Xeroxed information and no longer a totem of the underworld.

•   •   •

YOU CAN'T PROTECT your children from any of the things you imagine. You can cover the electrical outlets and buy bicycle helmets and secure spots at the top pediatrician and the top school. You can do every possible thing to ensure them a safe passage, to make sure that your money and power in the world are leveraged into their protection. But life is still coiled around them, full of terror and death and catastrophe.

As much as I love my sons, as quickly as I would lay down my life for them if the need arose, there is really only one thing I can protect them from.

The only thing you can protect your children from is the bad behavior of their parents.

The only thing I can promise my boys is that in this house the parents won't yell at each other or treat each other poorly. They won't become drunks or run off with lovers. In this house the parents will act like adults. They will take the children to church; they will set an example;

they will be present in every moment of their lives. Only death can part us from them.

In this house the mother will gladly surrender her beauty, her youth, any parts of her body that might pose a threat to the children by leaving them motherless. And the father will keep the place ticking along as close to normal as he can get it until she's on her feet. That's the only thing we can promise them for sure.

It turns out that many aspects of adult life that I have always considered complicated and messy and finely nuanced are in fact simple and clear-cut: life can be lived in pursuit of that elusive old dog, happiness, or it can be neatly fitted around obligation and sacrifice. Happiness may be a by-product of doing the right thing. But even if it's not, what matters — once you have had children, once you have decided to make a good life for them — is that you behave yourself.

When I was too sick to get out of bed, which was often, my husband took the children to school and to playdates and birthday parties. And when I couldn't walk from the car to the doctor's office, he carried me. And if that's a traditional marriage, I'll take it.

If a marriage is like a bank account, filled not only with affection but also with a commitment to the other person's well-being as much as to one's own, I suppose my balance was high. I suppose that all the days I had made a home for my husband, and all the times I had ended my writing days early so that he could work late or come home to a hot dinner and not to a scene of domestic chaos — all of that, as much as the desire and intensity that originally brought us together, were stores in my account. "Someone loves you," he would whisper to me when I was too sick to move. "Drink this," he would say, lifting my head for a swallow of water.

•   •   •

THOSE LIFE-AND-DEATH months of cancer treatment were the making of me as a mother. The previous five years I had been waiting for the big test to come along, the adrenaline surge that would make me strong enough to lift a car in a moment of crisis, or the long bout of croup that would keep me at the bedside night after night, listening to uneven breathing. Now it had come.

It took a long time to understand that I was no one's daughter anymore, and it took me just as long to really understand that I was a mother, not someone playing at homemaking.

Now, sick with chemotherapy, I couldn't look for my mother's help. I could only follow her old example: forge ahead, make the best of things, and don't frighten the children.

Once I stood with them on the hot asphalt parking lot outside a Payless shoe store and watched the field of cars shimmer and begin to break apart. If my mother had been there, she would have taken me home. But she wasn't there.

"Mom?"

"I'm fine. Let's go get some shoes!"

●   ●   ●

TODAY, AS I TYPE THIS, I'm well. My hair is back; my children are happy; my husband is starting to relax.

Here's what I know: When I woke up from the final surgery, I didn't want to see the articles I've written or the editors I've worked for. I wanted to see my sons and my husband. And I wanted to go home.

Acknowledgments

I share the achievement of this book with Ben Schwartz. He did all of the things that good editors do — he spent hours poring over my work and improving it, he championed everything I wrote, and he located the core of this book. But he also did something that only great editors can do: he believed in me so fiercely that I was forced to believe as well. When someone of Ben Schwarz's mind and erudition and literary taste thinks that you are a good writer, there is no turning back. He willed this book into being, and it is as much his as mine.

My late father, Thomas Flanagan, taught me everything I know. It was a sentimental education; it was a way of life. Every sentence of this book is influenced by the way he spoke and thought.

Bob Archer changed the way I read and hence the way I write. I am deeply grateful to him, as I am to Phil Holmes. Teaching English at Harvard-Westlake School was the best job I've ever had, and I am indebted to Bob and Phil, to my former colleagues, and to my students — grown up and scattered around the world, but fondly remembered.

I am grateful to the many people at the *Atlantic Monthly* with whom I have been honored to work, among them the late Mike Kelly, whom we all miss so dearly. I am also grateful to Ben, of course, to Cullen Murphy and Hilary McClellen and to the magazine's owner, David Bradley. I am indebted as well to the supremely talented staff of *The New Yorker*. David Remnick has encouraged and supported me, and I am forever in his debt. I am also grateful to Dana Goodyear, who shared her great understanding of *New Yorker* style with me and immeasurably tightened and polished my prose. Pam McCarthy has been a guardian angel. At Little, Brown, Reagan Arthur has been a true friend and daily cheerleader, and Michael Mezzo an appreciated friend. I am grateful, also, for the thoughtful work of Barb Jatkola and Katie Blatt, both of whom pored over the text, greatly improving it, and I am indebted to the woman who directed their work, the talented and gracious Peggy Freudenthal. My agent, Jennifer

Rudolph Walsh, has been fearless and protective, and I am grateful.

Peggy Burich Smith, Katherine Holmes-Chuba, Francie Norris, Tina Schwarz, and my sister Ellen Klavan are my inner circle, the five women whom I turn to for almost everything. I could not have written this book without them.

Before transferring to the nonfiction department of the Schwartz Writers' Program, I was a longtime student in its fiction writing division, working under the direction of bestselling author Christina Schwarz. Her careful and generous editing of my work prepared me well for the new direction, and I am eternally grateful.

I am grateful to the many thoughtful readers who advised and commented so helpfully along the way, in particular my friends Chris Cahill, Lisan Cooper, and Roberta Montgomery, as well as my mother-in-law, Connie Bell.

Amy Norman came up with the original subtitle for this book, and Linda Burstyn refined it. Both women are deeply appreciated. In the title department, I owe gratitude and apology to Robert Graves and Joan Didion.

I am grateful to Tom and Deedie Hudnut for looking after me in so many ways as I wrote this book.

Sarah Gold kept the project from overwhelming me.

Armando Guiliano and Barry Rosenbloom were

essential to the completion of the book. (Dead women tell no tales.)

Ellen, Drew, Spencer, and Faith are my family and my second home.

Patrick and Conor: We did it! Thanks for your excellent help and advice. I don't know why the publisher didn't call it "To Heck with All That," like we decided. I love you.

Rob: Here it is, the book you knew I could write. Granted, it's ten years overdue, but we've been so busy . . . happily so. Thank you.

Mom: So far, so good.

CAITLIN FLANAGAN is a staff writer at *The New Yorker* and a contributor to *The Atlantic Monthly*'s books section. She is a four-time finalist for the National Magazine Award, and her essays have appeared in *Best American Essays 2003* and *Best American Magazine Writing 2002, 2003,* and *2004.* She lives in Los Angeles with her family.